HERZL'S N

ONE LAND,

PETER RODGERS

CONSTABLE · LONDON

For FB

Constable & Robinson Ltd
3 The Lanchesters
162 Fulham Palace Road
London W6 9ER
www.constablerobinson.com

First published in Australia by Scribe Publications, 2004

First published in the UK by Constable,
an imprint of Constable & Robinson Ltd, 2005

A copy of the British Library Cataloguing in
Publication Data is available from the British Library.

ISBN 1-84529-167-0

Printed and bound in the EU

1 3 5 7 9 10 8 6 4 2

Contents

One hundred years of living painfully

Palestine is desolate and unlovely. And why should it be otherwise? Can the *curse* of the Deity beautify a land?
— Mark Twain, *Innocents abroad*

Palestine, by any yardstick, is less than prime real estate. Yet
to many millions — Jews, Christians, and Muslims — it
is 'Holy'. Within this land of abraded mountains and
gently undulating coastal plains they seek the same monotheistic
God: nourishing the soil with their blood as well as their
meditations, claiming a connection with it that precedes or
supersedes all others. From this land they glean an explanation
of what lies in the past and what will lie before them.

The land's embrace is one that some others cannot fathom.
Mark Twain, a visitor in 1868, described it as hopeless, dreary,
heart-broken: 'Over it broods the spell of a curse that has with-
ered its fields and fettered its energies'. He was equally unflatter-
ing about its inhabitants: the Arabs were a cunning, unhygienic
lot; orthodox Jews specialised in self-righteousness. Later, in the
early years after the First World War, a British General recorded

1

imperiously: 'I dislike them all equally ... a beastly people. The whole lot of them is not worth a single Englishman'.

Yet, to this day, Palestine and its people hold us all in firm embrace. No matter who we are, or where we are, the contest between Jew and Palestinian for this ancient land invades our daily consciousness. Our world is hostage to a struggle between less than one five-hundredth of its entire people. Even as we believe we are beyond surprise we are beguiled into pointless optimism, or shocked by fresh atrocity. Willingly or not, wittingly or not, we are drawn to look and to judge, to cajole and to plead. Often angry with despair we watch two intelligent, gifted peoples invoke the name of the 'great realtor in the sky', as Gore Vidal aptly put it, to lay exclusive claim upon this land and blight the life of the other.

And so it has been for the past century; a century in which the mix of national sentiment and religious conviction has proved especially lethal. A century which has seen many others pass across the landscape: Turks and Germans, French and British, Americans and Russians, offering advice and flattery, bribes and deceits, looking at once both powerful and impotent. For the singular truth of Palestine — that it must accommodate two worlds in one — has been incapable of resolution. Two worlds, two names — the Land of Israel versus the Land of Palestine — and two peoples: one waving the Old Testament as proof of ownership, the other chiding, 'But we belong here'.

Sifting through this hundred years of pain we see how little the dynamics of the conflict have changed; how eerily reminiscent today's antagonisms and falsehoods are of yesteryear's, how 'modern' leadership is anything but; how much today's self-righteous intransigence owes to what went before. All of us, it is true, are captives of our pasts. For Jews and Palestinians the result has been tragic — in the true, full meaning of the term, not the shallow, misleading way in which it is often applied nowadays to nothing more unfortunate than a sporting loss.

The story of Palestine in the past century has its share of political and military and human triumphs. But too often the dominant, recurring themes are those of lies and hypocrisies, myth-making and mutual demonisation; of a determined, energetic refusal to contemplate what it must be to be the other.

This story is told here more in sorrow than anger: sorrow for the continuing evil and indignity that Palestinians and Jews inflict on one another; sorrow for the way that the memory of all that went before continues to burden their lives; sorrow that daily inhumanity is the norm. The telling of the tale means criticism of both Jew and Palestinian — not for who they are but for what they have done, and for what they continue to do. It will, no doubt, draw fire from both sides. That, sadly, is part of the twisted logic of the conflict.

For each, guilt and innocence are absolutes, with malevolent behaviour always ascribed to the other — 'your side behaves appallingly, my side does not'. So too is criticism — 'if you criticise me you declare your blind allegiance to the other'. Thus criticism of Israeli[1] behaviour runs the gauntlet of the charge of 'anti-Semitism', while to criticise Palestinian behaviour is often cast as blind pro-Israeli 'bias'. Israelis (generally) and Palestinians (mostly) either cannot or will not acknowledge the plight of the other. All they can see is their own pain.

And on and on it goes, each side feeding off the ill-doing of the other to justify its own.

'Peace processes' have come and gone, some leaving a useful residue, others little more than new layers of hurt and thirst for revenge. No outsider has been able to provide the circuit-breaker. That should not surprise us — although so often it seems to. Peace cannot be imposed. It can only come from Jew and Palestinian. It has to occur within them and between them. It has to be driven by the level of disgust they feel about what they are doing to themselves, and to each other. It will have to challenge and to defeat the chilling logic of Auden's simple, despairing words:

I and the public know
What all schoolchildren learn,
Those to whom evil is done
Do evil in return.

That time is not yet with us — perhaps it never will be.

CHAPTER ONE

Herzl's 'new' Jew versus the 'semi-savage' native

If a time comes when our people in Palestine … push out the native inhabitants, these will not give up their place easily.

So wrote the Jewish writer Ahad Ha'am in 1891. Zionism was in its formative days and the dilemma emerging for its adherents would shape the history of the Holy Land and the globe ever after. The dilemma was two-fold: was there a local (non-Jewish) population in Palestine worthy of note; if so, how should the Zionists deal with it?

The answer to the first question should have been clear-cut. Anyone who knew anything about Palestine would have been keenly aware that, although the figures were imprecise, the country was anything but unpeopled. Ten years before Ha'am's revelatory comment, Palestine's population was some 460,000. Of these, around 400,000 were Muslim Arabs (the term Palestinian would not come into play for another generation); about 40,000 were Christian (mostly Greek Orthodox); and the remainder, Jews. Jerusalem's population was 30,000, about half of whom were Jewish.

How these figures challenge Zionism's powerful founding myth of 'a land without people for a people without a land'. There may have been a people without a land. But if there was a land without people it was certainly not Palestine.

Zionism, it is true, did not by definition mean the forced dispossession of Palestinian Arabs. 'We shall buy, buy, buy', declared Eliezer Ben-Yehuda, the pioneer of modern Hebrew. And large tracts of land were purchased legally from Arab 'notables', often residing comfortably in Beirut or elsewhere in the Arab world, for fledgling Jewish settlements. Such transactions enriched the notables and dispossessed many poor tenant farmers, who then found themselves competing with a growing Jewish labour movement for urban jobs. But Ben-Yehuda also made clear that deceit was afoot; that the country must be covertly, quietly conquered. 'We shall not set up committees so that the Arabs will know what we are after, we shall act like silent spies', he noted in the early 1880s.

How then did Theodor Herzl, who fathered political Zionism with his 30,000-word pamphlet, Der Judenstaat (The Jewish State), deal with the question of Palestine's Arabs? Easily — he simply ignored their existence, at least in public. There is not one single reference either to 'Arabs' or 'Palestinians' in this important tract. It was as if they did not exist, a convenience that other (though not all) Zionist leaders would happily follow. 'There are few things as egocentric as a revivalist movement', the contemporary Israeli writer and scholar Amos Elon has written. Zionist leaders moved in a strange twilight zone, 'seeing the Arabs and at the same time not seeing them'.

Herzl cuts a paradoxical figure. Born in Hungary into a comfortable, middle-class family, an assimilated Jew who spoke no Yiddish, Hebrew or Russian, for most of his life he showed little interest either in Jewry or the situation in Palestine. Herzl's epiphany came during the trial in the mid-1890s of a young, Jewish French military officer, Alfred Dreyfus. Framed on treason charges, Dreyfus was sent to the notorious Devil's Island penal colony. Covering the affair as the Paris correspondent for a Vienna daily newspaper, Herzl concluded that the anti-Semitism it unleashed was unerring proof that Jews had no future as 'assimilated' minorities in European states. The logical answer, indeed the only one, was a country of their own, where Jews could enjoy a security impossible anywhere else.

The Jewish State appeared in 1896. A year later, the first Zionist Congress, held in the Swiss town of Basel, declared that Zionism's aim was to create for the Jewish people 'a home in Palestine'. After the congress, Herzl confided to his diary, 'At Basel I founded the Jewish State. If I said this out loud today I would be answered with universal laughter. Perhaps in five years, certainly in fifty, everyone will know it.' What the comment lacked in humility it made up for in prophecy, as indeed did Herzl's foreboding about what the future held for European Jewry.

Herzl, certainly, was deeply conscious of the magnetic appeal of the Holy Land for many Jews. 'Palestine is our ever-memorable historic home', he wrote in *The Jewish State*. Jews had dreamt 'this kingly dream' of a state 'all through the long nights of their history. "Next year in Jerusalem" is our old phrase. It is now a question of showing that the dream can be converted into a living reality.' At first, Herzl was prepared to consider a homeland anywhere.[1] His overriding concern was the day-to-day reality of European Jewish life, of the need to get Jews out of Europe, not necessarily to Palestine. Jews living in the Russian Empire's 'Pale of Settlement' faced ongoing discrimination at best and, at worst, individual and state-organised violence. Many were keen to relocate, and the rise of Zionist thinking coincided with an exodus of eastern European Jewry. Their destination, paradoxically, was not the Holy Land but the USA. By the time the miscalculations of European leaders led them to war in 1914, one-third of eastern Europe's Jews — about two million people, or one-quarter of the world's total Jewish population — had made it to America. There, they would only ever constitute a small percentage of the total population. But their impact would be profound.

Increasingly obsessed with resolving the 'Jewish question', Herzl painted a halcyon picture of the would-be state. It would have no national language; rather, a 'federation of tongues' with everyone 'preserving the language in which their thoughts are at home'. 'Theocratic tendencies' would be kept in check, with the priesthood confined to the temple. In the same way, Herzl wrote, 'we shall keep our professional army within the confines of their barracks. Every man shall be as free and undisturbed in his faith or his disbelief as he is in his nationality.' The Promised Land would be a land of work, symbolised in its flag. 'I would suggest a white flag with seven gold stars,' Herzl commented, 'the white symbolises our pure, new life; the stars are the seven golden hours of the working day.' His 'new Jew' — whose mental muscles were already well developed through having to survive in discriminatory Europe — would now develop physical ones to make the land rich through 'labour and enterprise'. Later Zionist activists saw equally important non-agricultural uses for this new Jewish muscle. Moshe Smilansky declared in 1914: 'We are dealing here with a semi-savage people, who has extremely primitive concepts … If he senses in you power he will submit and will hide his hatred for you.'

After the Basel Congress of 1897, the rabbis of Vienna despatched a two-man fact-finding team to Palestine. In a famous phrase the travellers reported by cable that the bride was 'beautiful but married to another man'. The thought of Palestine's affections having already been claimed had little impact on Herzl. His focus, to continue the metaphor, switched to the bride's temporal father, hence his courtship of the sultan of Turkey — the decaying Ottoman Empire being still nominally in control of the Holy Land — and his overtures to others who might influence the wedding such as Kaiser Wilhelm, the King of Italy and Pope Pius X. Rebuffed in these endeavours, Herzl turned to Britain which, in 1903, offered a patch of colonial Uganda as a Jewish homeland. This triggered a heated debate between Zionist 'territorialists', who argued that anything was better than nothing, and the 'Zionists for Zion', for whom, as the name implies, it was Palestine or nothing. Herzl eventually sided with the latter. A year after his death in 1904 the Uganda offer was formally rejected at the Seventh Zionist Congress.

As much as he ever considered Palestine's local Arabs, Herzl concluded they would be the beneficiaries of what amounted to Zionism's *mission civilatrice*. The new state would help to form a European rampart against Asia, 'an outpost of civilisation as opposed to barbarism'. Zionists would form a guard of honour around the sanctuaries of Christendom, symbolising 'the solution of the Jewish Question after eighteen centuries of Jewish persecution'. Writing to the Arab notable, Yusuf Zia al-Khalidi, in 1899, Herzl argued that, rather than posing a threat to the Arab inhabitants of Palestine, the arrival of industrious, talented, well-funded Jews would benefit them materially. He pursued this theme in his later utopian novel *Altneuland* (*Old-New Land*). Set in a future Palestine (of 1923), Herzl created a world in which Zionism had brought progress and prosperity to, and cooperation with, the Arabs. Whatever the novel's literary shortcomings, its fiction was faultless.

As the fact of a substantial Arab majority in Palestine impinged on Zionist consciousness, in some eyes it heightened the need for subterfuge. But neither Zionist leaders nor the settlers making their way to the Holy Land wavered in their aims. One early settler wrote to his brother that the ultimate goal, in time, was to take over the Land of Israel and to make the Jews 'masters of their ancient homeland'. Some welcomed the opportunity to state openly and categorically what the contest was really about. For them, the Jewish tie to the Land of Israel (Eretz Yisrael) was paramount. The (re)creation of Israel represented the fulfilment of Biblical prophecy and the redemption of the Jewish past. Moshe Smilansky, for example, declared that the

Land of Israel either belonged to the Arabs who had settled there and then was 'lost to us', or it belonged to the Jewish people and 'our national interests come before all else'. Just in case the meaning was not clear he added, 'it is not possible for one country to serve as the homeland of two people'.

This view would be put with equal force by Ze'ev Jabotinsky, founder in the mid-1920s of the 'Revisionist' stream of Zionism. In a backhanded way this acknowledged the Arab presence with greater honesty than Herzl and his supporters had done. The Arabs might have been a 'yelling rabble dressed in savage-painted rugs' but at least they were 'a living people'. For them, Palestine would remain 'not a borderland, but their birthplace, the centre and basis of their own national existence'. Foreshadowing the approach later pursued by Ben-Gurion and still alive today, Jabotinsky's solution was to confront the Arabs until they gave up. 'As long as the Arabs preserve a gleam of hope that they will succeed in getting rid of us', he argued, 'nothing in the world can cause them to relinquish that hope.' The Arabs would yield 'only when they have given up all hope of getting rid of the alien settlers'. The tool for encouraging such acquiescence — and the emergence of moderate Arab voices with whom the Zionists could deal — would be an 'iron wall' of Jewish bayonets.

Drawing on the Bible and early Jewish history, many Zionists saw their claim to the land as far superior to any Palestinian one, based as it was on merely a few hundreds of years of attachment. Still, attachment it was, and wiser Jewish heads recognised the complications this posed for the Zionist dream. Delivering a lecture on the 'Arab Question' to the Zionist Congress in Basel in 1905, Yitzhak Epstein, a Russian-born teacher who had settled in Palestine in 1886, told his audience:

> We have forgotten one small matter. There is in our beloved land an entire nation, which has occupied it for hundreds of years and has never thought to leave … While we feel a deep love for the land of our forefathers, we forgot that the nation who lives in it today has a sensitive heart and loving soul. The Arab, like every man, is tied to his native land with strong bonds.

This was in marked contrast to the portrayal of Palestinian Arabs by many Jewish settlers as primitive, dishonest and lazy — by no means a dissimilar view of the 'natives' held by European colonists elsewhere. The convenience of this was to demean Palestinian nationalism, to cast it as a lesser version of the European and Jewish ideal. 'We have not come to an empty land to inherit it, but we have come to conquer a country from people inhabiting it, that governs it by the virtue of its language and savage culture', Moshe Shertok (later Sharett, and Israel's first foreign minister) opined in 1914. There was neither room nor thought of sharing. 'If we cease to look upon … the Land of Israel, as ours alone … all content and meaning will be lost to our enterprise.'

Palestinian Arabs saw an increasing Jewish presence in the Holy Land and reacted to it in various ways — with alarm, with hostility and occasional violence, with indifference. In the early 1890s a group of Jerusalem Arab notables sent a telegram to

Istanbul urging the grand vizier to halt Jewish immigration and to bar Jews from purchasing land. They complained that the Jews were taking 'all the lands out of the hands of the Muslims, taking all the commerce into their hands and bringing arms into the country'. Within a generation of the emergence of Zionism it was, without doubt, in competition with another national movement: more embryonic, certainly, but a growing challenge. In the eyes of some Zionists, the fact that Palestinian nationalism was a response to the growing Jewish presence rather than being something 'organic' made it inferior. But Jewish nationalism, too, had been fuelled by external factors — especially European anti-Semitism which had increased markedly after Czar Alexander III's ascent to the Russian throne in 1881.

The Zionists had a head start over their Palestinian rivals in ideas, determination and funding. They were way behind on demography, Jews still only forming a small proportion of Palestine's total population. They needed, as Herzl, had foreseen, the backing of a powerful friend. And there could, at the time, be no more powerful ally than Britain.

On 2 November 1917, after persistent lobbying from the future first president of Israel, Chaim Weizmann, the British cabinet agreed to the Balfour Declaration. Its critical section read:

His Majesty's government views with favour the establishment in Palestine of a national home for the Jewish people, and will use their best endeavours to facilitate the achievement of this object, it being clearly understood that nothing shall be done which may prejudice the civil and religious rights of existing non-Jewish communities in Palestine, or the rights and political status enjoyed by Jews in other countries.

Conveyed to Lord Rothschild in a letter signed by foreign secretary Balfour, this was a major triumph for Zionist diplomacy. However, concerned that it might damage their local standing (hence the observation about rights and political status), that the declaration made reference only to a national home, and that it was pregnant with potential confusion and contradiction, many Jews remained circumspect about the whole Zionist enterprise. The Jewish population of Palestine then stood at around 56,000, against an Arab population of 600,000. How could the achievement of a national 'home' for less than 10 per cent of the entire population not run a serious risk of prejudicing the civil and religious, not to mention the political, rights of the other 90 per cent?

These qualifications and contradictions mattered little to Weizmann, whose belief in the justness of the Jewish claim to Palestine and determination to create a Jewish state there were unshakeable. At the Paris Peace Conference he stated famously that a Jewish 'national home' meant making Palestine 'as Jewish as England is English'. But he also recognised the need for caution, indeed subterfuge, if this goal were to be realised. The year after Balfour, Weizmann led a Zionist delegation to Palestine. Ormsby Gore, the British political officer attached to the delegation, recorded him as telling the British high commissioner in Cairo — who had commented on Arab fears of a Jewish state and the expulsion of the Arabs — that the Zionists 'had no intention whatsoever of expropriating or displacing the Arab population of Palestine or of seeking to set up a Jewish State or Government in the near future'. Weizmann pursued this line during a subsequent meeting in Jerusalem with the influential al-Husseini family. He claimed it was 'no part of his aim to establish anything in the nature of a Jewish State or Jewish Government' after the end of the war. Rather, he and his colleagues 'were anxious to see established an Administration, in his personal view, preferably a British Administration, under which Jew and Arab could work harmoniously for the development of the country on a basis of equality and justice'.

Gore's summation was that the Arabs were apprehensive about expropriation and the loss of their social and political prestige, while the Jews were 'frightened of Arab fanaticism, intrigue and attempts at domination'. Gore made no secret of his own sympathies. In an April 1918 letter to the secretary of the war cabinet, Maurice Hankey, he commented, 'If this splendid country is ever to be properly developed and still more if it is ever to be British, it is only the Zionists who can accomplish these two aims'.

Three decades later the British would be gone, the Palestinians and their Arab allies would be in disarray, and David Ben-Gurion would declare the creation of a Jewish state in Palestine. But the state to which Herzl claimed paternity, which marked the fulfilment of the Zionist dream, came at terrible cost — to both the Jewish and Palestinian peoples. That cost is still being paid.

CHAPTER TWO

Zionism triumphant

O ne thing that ruling powers should know is how many people they have under their sway. So, being awarded a 'mandate' over Palestine by the newly formed League of Nations, Britain did a head count of its new territory in the early 1920s. The census put Palestine's population at just under 760,000. Of these, some 663,000 were Muslim or Christian Palestinians, and the remainder Jewish.

These figures posed a challenge for Britain. To distinguish mandates from pseudo-colonial ventures, it had been given Palestine in 'trust', to be administered for the good of its people. But which ones? Palestine's Arab and Jewish communities, and their external backers, viewed the country from very different ends of the telescope. Where were the British supposed to look? And in the Balfour Declaration they had, after all, committed themselves to *something* Jewish in Palestine.

Faced with these hard choices, the British tried hard to shut their eyes and hope for the best. But Palestine, as they should have known, is not a place where the best often happens, at least in modern times. After three decades of tacking between Arab and Jew, of occasionally pleasing and just as often displeasing both, the British sailed away. But they had planted, in the late 1930s, the seed of dividing the 'Holy Land' between Jew and Palestinian. And as this seed grew, so did another, more furtively perhaps because of its capacity to taint Zionism's moral message of 'return' and 'redemption'. This was the idea of the 'transfer' of Palestine's Arab population. The rationale for this reflected two layers in the bedrock of Zionist thinking. The first involved a denial that Palestine had a 'native' population worth worrying about. The second layer — crucial when the first one had been drilled through — was the argument that this 'native' population was really only part of the wider Arab world. It could, therefore, happily be shifted to that world. No one, it seems, thought to ask the Palestinians, resident in the Holy Land longer than Europeans had been in America, what they thought of the idea.

The notion of 'transfer' bobbed around in Zionist thinking from the start. When he was not arguing for the material benefits that would accrue to Arab Palestinians from the Zionist enterprise, or in denial of their very existence, Herzl certainly entertained the idea of relocation. In 1895, a year before the publication of *The Jewish State*, he wrote in his diary of 'spiriting the penniless population' across the border 'discreetly and circumspectly'.

David Ben-Gurion, who as head of the Zionist movement would take Herzl's dream to fruition, displayed — to put it gently — a flexible approach to 'transfer'. During the First World War he wrote: 'We do not intend to push the Arabs aside, to take their land, or to disinherit them'. Some two decades later, however, with Palestinian Arabs, Jews, and the British at loggerheads and another world war looming he wrote to his son, Amos: 'We must expel the Arabs and take their places ... and if we have to use force ... we have force at our disposal'.

Two factors had worked on Ben-Gurion. Following anti-Jewish riots in 1920, 1921, and 1929, a full-scale Arab revolt against British rule and the Zionist enterprise erupted in 1936. It smouldered for the next three years. In May 1936, Ben-Gurion told the Jewish Executive Agency: 'We both want the same thing: we both want Palestine. And that is the fundamental conflict.' The second factor was the British response to the Arab revolt in the form of the 1937 royal commission, named after its chairman, Lord Peel. Foreshadowing the nature of the British retreat a decade later, both from Palestine and the Indian subcontinent, the report concluded that the only hope lay in partition. It recommended the creation of two states: a Jewish one of a mere 5,000 square kilometres, or about 20 per cent of the country; the remainder would become an Arab state, except for a British-controlled enclave linking the port of Jaffa with Jerusalem. Jewish immigration would be limited to 12,000 a year.

We can only wonder now how different the history of pre- and post-war Palestine, and of European Jewry, might have been if the proposal had been given a chance by both sides. Arab Palestinians were seemingly unable to comprehend both the 'push' and 'pull' factors driving Zionism — a growing anti-Semitism in Europe which climaxed in the Nazi persecution of the Jews, and Jewish attachment to the land of Biblical Israel.

Affronted by the notion of partition, the Palestinians rejected it out of hand. The Zionist response was more measured and more complex, carrying overtones of the 'all-or-nothing' division over tactics triggered by Britain's 'Uganda offer' in 1903. The pro-partition camp argued that, whatever the size of the Jewish state, it was a start. For Jabotinsky's revisionists, and those of his ilk, it was all or none of Biblical Israel. After considerable wrangling, the pro-partitionists won the day. But Ben-Gurion made it clear, privately, that this was merely a start. He wrote to his son Amos:

> I am certain we will be able to settle in all the other parts of the country, whether through agreement … with our Arab neighbours or in another way. Erect a Jewish State at once, even if it is not the whole land. The rest will come in the course of time. It must come.

How words come back to haunt us. Today, it is precisely the fear of such incrementalism — on the part of Palestinians — that makes so many Israelis leery about any agreement with them. For Ben-Gurion, Peel's mini-state was only a beginning, the springboard to achieve Zionism's larger aims. Would a Palestinian mini-state now be any different? Israelis have their own example to fear.

Territorial compromise was a painful reality for many in the Zionist camp, unthinkable for those in the Arab one. But Jewish pragmatists, led by Weizmann and Ben-Gurion, established partition as the way forward. And in one other vital way Peel also gave the Zionists heart. The report recommended the 'voluntary' transfer of the substantial Arab population living in the intended Jewish state, and held out the prospect of a compulsory population 'exchange'. This was certainly a step in the right direction, even for those hardliners dissatisfied over the size of the proposed Jewish state. In typically hard-nosed fashion, Jabotinsky made clear his approach to transfer when he wrote to a supporter in November 1939 that American Jewry should be 'instructed' to raise half a billion dollars to assist Iraq and Saudi Arabia absorb the Palestinian Arabs. There was no choice, he asserted: 'the Arabs must make room for the Jews of Eretz Israel'.

Like deadlines, however, war has a great way of concentrating the mind. The Peel Report had hardly been grudgingly accepted by the Zionist leadership before the British began to unpick the notion of partition. The approaching conflict with Nazism brought home sharply the fact that Britain needed the backing of the Arab and Muslim worlds more than it needed Jewish support. A government White Paper issued in May 1939 effectively halted British support for the Zionist cause and — by extension — for a Jewish state. The paper went to some length to show that Britain was sensitive to Jewish aspirations. It had honoured the requirement 'to facilitate Jewish immigration under suitable conditions'. Under British rule the Jewish population of 'the national Home' had risen to some 450,000, 'approaching a third of the entire population of the country'. But, the paper added, the framers of the mandate in which the Balfour Declaration was embodied 'could not have intended that Palestine should be converted into a Jewish State against the will of the Arab population of the country'. So it was 'not part of the policy' of His Majesty's Government that this should come about.

In words that now seem eerily prophetic, the White Paper — a curious brew of idealism, pragmatism and cynicism — warned of the risk of 'a fatal enmity' between Jew and Palestinian, of the situation in Palestine becoming 'a permanent source of friction between all peoples in the Near and Middle East'. The answer to this was a policy enabling further Jewish immigration only with Arab agreement. A total of 75,000 Jews would be allowed to migrate to Palestine during the following five years. After then, immigration would not be permitted unless the Arabs of Palestine were 'prepared to acquiesce in it'. The two peoples in Palestine, the paper chided, 'must learn to practise mutual tolerance, goodwill and cooperation', adding unnecessarily, 'His Majesty's Government is not blind to the fact that some events of the past make the task of creating these relations difficult'.

Undeterred by what they saw around them on a near-daily basis the British envisaged an independent Palestine within ten years. The two peoples would share authority in government to ensure that the 'essential interests' of each community were protected. The only thing the mandatory power got right, almost, was the time frame. Shared authority was anathema both to the Zionists and their Arab opponents. The British well knew this. Their sense of judgement and responsibility was that of a sleepwalker in an antique shop.

The Zionist leadership had good cause for anger over the

White Paper. But they were in a quandary. It was a natural ally of the British war effort, yet an opponent of the new British approach to Palestine. Ben-Gurion's solution was typically pragmatic: 'We will fight the war against Hitler as if there were no White Paper; we will fight the White Paper as if there were no war'. The war — and its terrible consequences for European Jewry — ultimately made the Zionist cause unassailable. Herzl's message all along had been that the Jews had no future in Europe, that only a Jewish state could protect the Jewish people. In the words of Benny Morris, one of Israel's leading 'revisionist' historians,[1] 'the Holocaust mobilized, as nothing else could, the support of world Jewry ... the guilty conscience of Christendom translated into support for Zionism'. Meanwhile the Palestinian leadership had been stained by its collusion with the Axis powers against the allied cause.[2]

In the late 1930s the British put the partition of the Holy Land and the transfer of people on their official agenda. These ideas had gotten nowhere before World War II put them on the international agenda and ensured that they did. With Britain making clear that it wanted out, on 29 November 1947 the General Assembly of the newly created United Nations passed Resolution 181, endorsing the UN special committee on Palestine's report recommending partition. It called 'upon the inhabitants of Palestine to take such steps as may be necessary ... to put this plan into effect' and appealed 'to all Governments and all peoples to refrain from taking any action which might hamper or delay the carrying out of these recommendations'. Thirty-three countries voted in favour of the resolution, including the USA and the

Soviet Union. Thirteen voted against, made up of ten Muslim states plus Cuba, Greece and India. Ten countries abstained, including Britain.

For the Zionist cause, the UN's approach was a marked improvement over the Peel Report. The proposed Jewish state would encompass some 57 per cent of mandatory Palestine, compared with 20 per cent under Peel. Demographically, though, it would be a nightmare. Nearly 50 per cent of its one million population would be Arab. Despite this, and for all its seeming contradictions, Resolution 181 represented a diplomatic triumph for the mainstream Zionist leadership. But the contest still had a long way to run. The Palestinians, represented by the Arab Higher Committee, dismissed the partition plan as 'absurd, impracticable and unjust'. A new phase of the Zionist enterprise — with propaganda, mutual demonisation, Arab-Jewish violence, and Jewish military prowess on centre stage — was in the making. The challenge against partition came not just from the Palestinians but also from hardline elements within the Zionist movement.

Hardly had the ink dried on Resolution 181 than Menachem Begin, commander of the Etzel militia (an acronym of National Military Organisation), and a future Israeli prime minister, declared that partition was illegal. 'It will never be recognised ... Jerusalem was and will forever be our capital. Eretz Yisrael will be restored to the people of Israel. All of it ... forever.' As the clock ticked away on the British mandate, Begin's militia, with the support of the mainstream Jewish force the Haganah, attacked the village of Deir Yassin, near Jerusalem, leaving scores of Palestinians, including women and children, dead. This event remains one of the most acrimonious in the many instances of Jewish-Arab violence. Was the attack a premeditated attempt at 'ethnic cleansing' or a legitimate military response? The Jewish Agency hastened to condemn the attack, but Begin saw only good coming from it. The 'legend of terror' that it spread among Arab civilians and troops 'seized with panic at the mention of Irgun soldiers', he said, was 'worth a half a dozen battalions to the force of Israel'. Why? Because the example of Deir Yassin helped the fledgling Jewish state achieve demographic comfort.

On 14 May 1948, with a picture of Theodor Herzl gazing down upon him, Ben-Gurion read the statement proclaiming the new State of Israel. Its borders were left undefined. This was no oversight, but a tactic for possible future expansion beyond the UN's partition plan. The US, under president Truman, extended immediate *de facto* recognition. It was quickly topped by the Soviet Union's *de jure* recognition. Israel's immediate challenge, however, lay not in garnering international support but in overcoming the military threat from its Arab neighbours.

Failing to cope with the pace of events, overestimating their own capacities and underestimating the strength of Jewish resolve, the new state's Arab neighbours decided it should be strangled at birth. Egypt's King Farouk prematurely celebrated his conquest of Palestine by issuing a set of commemorative postage stamps. It must have been especially galling that his was the first Arab nation to sign a formal armistice agreement with Israel, in February 1949. Lebanon, Jordan and Syria followed suit. By July of that year the first Israeli-Arab war was officially over. It had claimed the lives of nearly 1 per cent of the entire Jewish population of some 650,000 but Israel's nationalist myths would thrive on its victorious 'war of independence'. It now controlled almost 80 per cent of mandated Palestine, four times the amount allocated under Peel, and a 25 per cent improvement over the UN partition plan. It had outwitted and outgunned its opponents, expelling all but the Jordanian Arab Legion, which held on to the West Bank and East Jerusalem. The new state was a force to be reckoned with.

Zionism's triumph became the Palestinian *nakbah*, or catastrophe. By the time the war ended some 700,000 Palestinians had left Israel. And 'left' had become one of the most contentious words in the lexicon of the Jewish-Palestinian conflict. Many Palestinians, without doubt, fled to preserve their lives. Many, without doubt, were expelled at gunpoint. Whatever the precise cause of individual departure, whatever the precise balance between those who 'jumped' and those who were 'pushed', the Palestinian exodus — involving some 80 per cent of Palestinians living in what became Israel — was unqualified good news for the new Jewish state. Weizmann described it as 'a miraculous simplification of the problem'.

Never comprehending the strength of Jewish attachment to the Land of Israel, never understanding the historical and social forces at work outside Palestine, the Palestinian leadership, such as it was, stuck its head in the sand. Zionism was a bad dream. Ignored for long enough, it would burn off like a desert mist. To compound the disaster, the Palestinian leadership got into bed with the Nazis at the very time they were slaughtering European

Jews. Then, as Arab Palestine crumbled about them, leaders got out while the going was good. Hussein Khalidi, secretary of the Arab Higher Committee, complained that 'Everyone has left me … Everyone who has … some money — off he goes to Egypt, to Lebanon, to Damascus.' Abba Eban would later offer the memorable comment that the Arabs 'never missed an opportunity to miss an opportunity'. The glib humour of this remark disguised a host of complexities of which Eban, as one of Israel's most gifted statesmen, would have been well aware. *If* the Palestinians had accepted the Peel partition plan; *if* they and the Arab states had accepted the UN partition plan, the region and the world might have been a very different place. It is only *might*. Looking back now, there was a seeming inevitability about the nationalist and historical forces that brought Jew and Arab into competition and conflict over a land which mattered so deeply to them both.

The catastrophe was only partly of Palestinian making. Whatever the flirtations of the Palestinian leadership with Hitler, the Palestinians could not be held accountable for the Nazis' decimation of European Jewry. Yet it was knowledge of that decimation that turned the tide in favour of Zionism, and that led inexorably to the uprooting of Palestinian society. And uprooting it was. Historians and others will argue to the end of days about its causes — the extent to which the Palestinians ran or were driven away at gunpoint; whether Deir Yassin was a local incident or part of a carefully plotted strategic plan. It hardly mattered to the outcome. Yet even after this 'relocation', which reduced Israel's non-Jewish population to around 20 per cent of the total, unease remained about the Arab minority.

Yitzhak Ben-Tzvi, who would later serve ten years as Israeli president, told a meeting of the Labour Secretariat early in 1949 that 'there are too many Arabs in the country'. His concerns were echoed a few months later by MP Shlomo Lavi: 'The large number of Arabs in the country worries me. The time may come when we will be a small minority in the State of Israel.' A fellow Labour MP put the issue more forcefully: 'I'm not willing to accept a single Arab, and not only an Arab but any gentile. I want the State of Israel to be entirely Jewish.' A prominent labour leader noted that his enjoyment of the landscape between Tel Aviv and Haifa was helped by the fact that there was 'not a single Arab to be seen'.

In little more than half a century Zionism had scored a spectacular triumph of Israel recreated, of a state for the Jews. It was a triumph achieved, however, on the bones of millions of European Jews, and at the expense of Palestinian society and of Palestinian nationalism. It was a triumph which would prove illusory in bringing to the Jewish people the peace and security that they had clamoured for, which Theodor Herzl had held before them. Whatever their emotional attachment to the land they now ruled, whatever their historical claim to it, the Jews of Israel had supplanted another people — who would not forget.

CHAPTER THREE

This land is my land; your land is my land . . .

I saiah Berlin once observed cryptically that Israel always had 'more history than geography'. Six days of fighting in June 1967 dramatically changed that. The product of human bluff and misjudgement at its best (or worst), the war lasted less than a week, left some 50,000 dead or injured, uprooted over 300,000 Palestinians and decimated the military capability of Israel's Arab neighbours. In late May, Egypt's ebullient president Nasser had declared that Israel's very existence was 'an aggression'. He was going to put an end to it. The war effectively ended him politically, though he lingered on until 1970 when a heart attack permanently removed him from the scene. Asked what would happen to 'native' Israelis (that is, Jews born in Palestine) after the inevitable, forthcoming Arab victory, the Palestine Liberation Organisation (PLO) head, Ahmed Shukeiry, generously noted that they could stay on. He estimated, however, that none 'will survive'.

Israel fought what it portrayed as a defensive, existential war. The enormous territorial and population disparities between the opposing sides lent itself readily to a David and Goliath characterisation. After all, according to the Old Testament, the shepherd boy and the giant had slugged it out in the Elah valley,

29

just to the south-west of Jerusalem. The 'Six Day War' covered a much wider area geographically. But, again, the result was a stunning knockout victory for the shepherd. In less than a week, Israel trebled the territory under its control: it captured the vast tract of the Sinai as well as the millstone of the Gaza Strip from Egypt; seized the strategically valuable Golan Heights from Syria, and evicted the Jordanians from East Jerusalem and the West Bank. The entire 'Land of Israel' now lay in Jewish hands, ready for redemption.

Some interpreted this as a divine miracle. Admiration and funds flooded in from the Jewish Diaspora, captured in the remark that 'Israel was they; now Israel is we'. New heroes emerged and new myths sprouted. One of these heroes, defence minister Moshe Dayan, became, according to one wry comment, 'the best-known Jew since Jesus Christ'. Dayan reportedly went on to advise America's General Westmoreland, then struggling in the Vietnam sinkhole, that the surest way of winning a war was to 'pick the Arabs as your enemy'.

But as the events of 1948 created a new state and new dilemmas, so did the war of 1967. Believers in the messianic notion of Greater Israel had good reason to think that the Lord had delivered. What they did not realise at first was that His package contained several very sharp thorns. What was Israel to do with its new territories and its newfound power? Even more, what was it to do with the subjugated Palestinian population? Foresight is a rare commodity in both individuals and nation states. In post-1967 Israel, flush with new territory and nationalist fervour, it was largely absent.

Largely, though not entirely. Having witnessed the expulsion of Palestinian villagers in the Latrun salient shortly after the war, the novelist Amos Keenan, then serving in the army, wrote: 'The children walking in the streets, bitter with tears, will be the fedayin [guerillas] ... in the next round. Today we lost our victory.' Later, Nahum Goldman, for many years the president of the World Jewish Congress, observed that every military victory by Israel had resulted in new political difficulties 'particularly the incredibly quick victory in the Six Day War'. Israel, he suggested, risked 'winning itself to death'.

The issues after 1967 essentially were the same as those confronted by the early Zionists — land and the presence of a non-Jewish population. The response was remarkably similar: pretend either that the Palestinians were largely non-existent, in spite of the overwhelming demographic evidence to the contrary, or that they did not matter. If they did not matter, could there really be any harm in taking their land? Clearly the answer was no. So prime minister Golda Meir famously taunted: 'Who are the Palestinians? I am a Palestinian.' This was an imaginative claim, to say the least, for someone born in Russia.

A later (fellow) prime minister, Yitzhak Shamir, was even less accommodating. The PLO were 'two-legged beasts of prey, thirsting for Jewish blood'. Shamir's defenders argued that he was in fact referring to Palestinian 'terrorists'. If nothing else, this should have underlined the definitional minefield over 'terrorism'. Shamir had played a leading part in the 1946 bomb attack on the King David hotel in Jerusalem, then the British military headquarters, which had left some 90 people, including civilians, dead.

Israel, post-1967, was the unquestioned regional super-power. It could have used this might in two sharply contrasting ways: to fulfil the Zionist dream of Jews in the entire land of Biblical Israel, or to try to extract a land for peace deal, not just with the Palestinians but the wider Arab world. It chose, in effect, the muddle way. With the exception of Jerusalem, on which there was a singularity of purpose — that it be made irretrievably Jewish — policy towards the occupied territories was often incoherent and contradictory, lacking both imagination and wisdom. Abba Eban may well have been right about Arabs missing opportunities. It was an observation he might equally have applied to his own people. Israeli actions (especially the colonisation of occupied Palestinian territory) did as much as anything else to continue, complicate and enflame the conflict.

The best insights into this come not from outside analysis but from Israelis themselves. Amos Elon has commented that the 'Israeli colonial intrusion into the West Bank came in fairly shadowy/absentminded circumstances. Few people took it seriously at first. Some deluded themselves that it was bound to be temporary.' The Israeli parliament never voted on a settlement project, but the squatters 'were gradually legalised, lavishly subsidised, and eventually hailed as national heroes'. Take also the comments by Michael Ben-Yair, attorney general in the Rabin government of the mid-1990s. He wrote in 2002:

The Six-Day War was forced on us; however the war's seventh day, which began on June 12, 1967 and has continued to this day, is the product of our choice. We enthusiastically chose to become a colonial society, ignoring international treaties, expropriating lands, transferring settlers from Israel to the occupied territories, engaging in theft and finding justifications for all these activities. Passionately desiring to keep the occupied territories we developed two judicial systems: one — progressive, liberal — in Israel; and the other — cruel, injurious — in the occupied territories. In effect, we established an apartheid regime in the occupied territories immediately after their capture. That oppressive regime exists to this day.

Those who exercised political power in Israel after 1967 often showed the same disdain for the Palestinians exhibited by many of the early Zionists. Their attachment to land could never match that of the Jews. Their dreams of nationhood could be dismissed as inferior — a response to Zionism's energy and purpose rather than a natural, evolving phenomenon. As much as there was a Palestinian 'issue', the Palestinians could be bought off. Give them a basic job and a roof over their heads and they would be quieted — they burned neither with aspirations nor ideals. Samuel Katz, a Begin propagandist, would argue that the Jews of Israel, as a 'dynamic people', required additional living space to support their expansion. Arabs and Palestinians, by contrast, were 'amorphous abstracts without any legitimate claim to nationhood or peoplehood'. Their 'plunder' of the Land of Israel had been put to an end 'only when the Jews began to settle there'.

The Israeli approach might have been dismissive, but it was also fearful. And it was this fear that drove the settlement movement. The tragic irony is that the more energised this movement became the greater the reason for Israeli fear. Settlements became a drug of addiction; it seems inconceivable that Israelis and their governments could not recognise that the expropriation of Palestinian land could be anything but harmful. But like an alcoholic easing fear of cirrhosis by having another Scotch, the Israeli reaction to Palestinian anger over settlements was to build more of them.

The first Israeli settlement was built not on Palestinian land but on Syrian. On 15 July 1967, barely a month after the Six Day War had ended, a party of settlers linked to the kibbutz movement of the labour minister, Yigal Allon, took up residence in an abandoned Syrian army camp near the town of Quneitra. Their presence was quickly and favourably acknowledged by the government, and Kibbutz Meron Hagolan was born. According to Shlomo Gazit, coordinator of Israeli government operations in the occupied territories between 1967 and 1974, the official motive in allowing a civilian presence on the Golan was 'to take care of the abandoned Syrian livestock, to harvest the grain and pick the fruit'.

Some four decades later Israeli settlers were still tending the cattle and the orchards. For the settlement movement would be driven by a good deal more than cows and crops. Yigal Allon argued that a security border that was not a state border was a misnomer. And a state border not settled 'along its length by Jews was not a security border'. This view was echoed by the formidable Golda Meir, who declared that the 'frontier is where Jews live, not where there is a line on a map'. Moshe Dayan saw settlements as providing the essential rationale for a continuing Israeli military presence in the occupied territories. Without the settlements 'we cannot keep the army in the territories'; without them, the Israeli Defence Force (IDF) 'would be a foreign army ruling a foreign population'.

Shlomo Gazit has written that settlements were designed 'to establish a new reality' that would influence the future political situation. They were built in places 'from which Israel had no intention of withdrawing'. Pressure groups pointed to the importance of settlements achieving a variety of goals, identified by Gazit as:

- Determining future borders.
- Bargaining chips: settlements would force the Arab leaders to reconsider their positions and convince them that time was not unlimited. The longer they postponed 'the less negotiable land would be left'.
- Laying the groundwork for Israeli-Palestinian cooperation; in effect, imposing 'co-existence' upon the parties.
- Tying Israel's hands: any government would be less free in its negotiating approach if the army's withdrawal from certain areas also meant the evacuation of civilian settlements.
- Messianic: from the outset of the Zionist movement settling in the Land of Israel and building new settlements were sacred tenets.

On occasion, some messianically minded settlers debunked

the security rationale — arguing that they were doing God's business and no one else's. Kiryat Arba, established in September 1968 on land confiscated from Palestinian residents of Hebron, became an important marker in the fight for 'Biblical Israel'. It was also a stepping-stone in the pursuit of Jewish claims for a presence in Hebron itself, the burial place of Abraham and of intense religious significance to both Jew and Muslim. In early 1980, an advance guard from Kiryat Arba took over several abandoned buildings in the centre of Hebron. Gazit has commented:

> Thus the seed of the disaster of the existence of a fanatical Jewish settlement in the middle of a radical Moslem town was sown. This created a flash point ... culminating in the massacre by Baruch Goldstein in the Cave of the Patriarchs.

Goldstein, a Brooklyn-born resident of Kiryat Arba, murdered 29 Palestinians at prayer in Hebron in 1994. He is memorialised in the settlement in a way sickeningly reminiscent of Palestinian acclaim of their own terrorist 'martyrs'.

Mostly, there was a happy crossover between the security and messianic arguments. Menachem Begin, swept into power in 1977 at the head of a Likud-led government, declared that the right of the people 'to the land of ancestors cannot be separated from its right to peace and security'. Geoffrey Aronson, a historian of the settlement movement, has written that after Begin came to power 'the ideology of Greater Israel and the practical imperatives of domestic policy were synthesized into a dynamic policy of colonization'. Begin, Aronson noted, devoted his life to the struggle for Jewish control over Palestine. In 1947, his movement had sent a memorandum to the United Nations declaring that:

> the partition of the land of Israel is illegal. This country, the eternal homeland of our people, is historically, geographically, and economically one unit. Is it not absurd that the administration of Judea, Samaria [the West Bank], and the Galilee should be in the hands of non-Jews? Our people will wage a battle until every square inch of our land is liberated.

In the early 1980s, Begin told the Israeli parliament that if Jewish settlement in Palestine in the late nineteenth century was moral, settlement throughout the entire land of Biblical Israel was similarly moral. An intriguing, if largely academic, exercise is to reverse the point: if post-1967 settlement in the occupied territories is immoral or at least misguided — which almost everyone except the Israelis believes is the case — what does this say about the morality or legality of early Zionist settlements?

The apparent inability of settlement advocates to imagine that the natives might become (even more) restless as they watched the post-1967 Israeli land-grab reminds us of the attitudes shown towards the Palestinians by many early Zionists. Ariel Sharon, then defence minister, declared in 1982: 'I believe that one day, and this day is not far off, calm will return to the Golan Heights, Judea and Samaria and we can fulfil our desires in peace and security'. We can only wonder what he was smoking at the time. Or perhaps this was merely

Ben-Gurion's assessment of Sharon at work — a brilliant soldier, but 'very economical' with the truth.

Where the natives' restlessness, actual or potential, was in fact recognised, the answer was to swamp the Palestinian population with a Jewish one. A 1980 report by Mattityahu Drobless, the co-chair of the World Zionist Organization's settlement department, declared:

Being cut off by Jewish settlements the minority population will find it difficult to form a territorial and political continuity. There mustn't be even the shadow of a doubt about our intention to keep the territories of Judea and Samaria for good. Otherwise, the minority population may get into a state of growing disquiet which will eventually result in recurrent efforts to establish an additional Arab state in these territories. The best and most effective way of removing every shadow of a doubt about our intention to hold on to Judea and Samaria forever is by speeding up the settlement momentum in these territories.

'Minority population?' At that time there were possibly 20,000 settlers in the West Bank, compared to a Palestinian population approaching one million. But the times were auspicious, and hope was at hand in the form of Sharon. For him there was no West Bank. It was Judea and Samaria. There was no East Jerusalem, only Jerusalem. And, in the tradition of both early and later hardline Zionism, there were certainly no Palestinians. In 1977, as minister for agriculture — through which he controlled the Israeli Lands Authority and therefore all state and public land — Sharon unveiled a 'Vision for Israel at Century's End'. This envisaged two million Jews settling in the occupied territories by the year 2000. As an ardent advocate of 'genuine Zionism', Sharon later spoke of 'massive settlement all over the West Bank' as the best answer 'to the various plans that outsiders are trying to foist on Israel'.

He and others had learnt well from the Zionist experience in Palestine. Settlement led to sovereignty — not necessarily this day, this year, or even this decade. But it was sovereignty that would come as surely as the sun rose each day over the crumpled Judean hills. The proposition, as Aronson has suggested, was simple: 'If enough Jewish settlements could be established and enough land seized and placed under Jewish control, the Palestinians would wake up one day to discover that they had lost their country'. Under Sharon's patronage, more than 60 settlements had been established in the West Bank by the early 1980s. At first they were anything but grand, but they were the all-important 'facts on the ground'.

The bond between messianic idealism and the security of the Jewish state — epitomised by Begin and Sharon — was conspicuous on the Israeli right. But it held no mortgage. It is important to remember that the first ten years of settlement activity took place under Labour governments, whose luminaries included Moshe Dayan, Golda Meir, Yitzhak Rabin, and Shimon Peres. Aronson has noted that defence minister Peres, like his predecessor Dayan, 'supported colonisation throughout the West Bank', and argued that Jews had the right to settle in both Judea and Samaria.

In one instance, Peres directed the defence forces to help those trying to establish a new settlement near Nablus in order 'to embarrass Rabin [then in his first stint as prime minister] and raise questions about his leadership'. No doubt, this episode played a part in shaping Rabin's view of Peres as an 'indefatigable subverter'. For his own part Rabin, by the end of his first period as prime minister in 1977, had, in the words of the Israeli academic, Yaron Ezrahi, 'yielded to the nationalist, religious Gush Emunim's[1] determination ... Their appeal in welding Zionist rhetoric with messianic religious fervour proved almost irresistible'.

As the crow flies, the distance from the conspicuously 'secular' city of Tel Aviv to the West Bank religious settlement of Beit El, north of Jerusalem, where Jacob dreamed of a ladder reaching unto Heaven, is a less than arduous journey. As time flies, it is at least 2000 years. Beit El's settlers, like those in other religious outposts, believed they were doing God's work. This is a hard argument to toss. After all, anyone who reads the Old Testament will know that in Numbers 33: 52–53 God directed the Jews to 'take possession of the land and settle in it', dispossessing all other inhabitants in the process. Just what those other inhabitants had done to deserve such a fate — in perpetuity — was not clear and, certainly, not all Old Testament pronouncements were taken so literally. But the Biblical directive that the land was exclusively Jewish provided the vital philosophical cloak for the settlement movement.

That said, the practical imperatives — a heady mix of political and security considerations — were never far from sight. A

West Bank dotted with Israeli settlements would make for a very unlikely Palestinian state. It would ensure that any process of Palestinian 'self-rule' would be highly fragmented and ineffectual. Drobless had written that the disposition of Israeli settlements must be carried out 'not only around the settlement of the minorities [that hopeful and entirely misleading term again] but also in between them'. Israel was there to stay, come hell or high water, regardless of international pressure, peace processes, or the strictures of international law.

In July 1977, the US president, Jimmy Carter, appealed to the newly elected Likud government under Menachem Begin to freeze settlement activity. There were then some 50,000 Israelis living in East Jerusalem, annexed by Israel shortly after the Six Day War, but only around 7,000 in the West Bank and the Gaza Strip combined. Begin ignored the request. Two months later Sharon unveiled his 'vision' of two million settlers by the century's end. For the next quarter of a century, various US administrations would make appeals similar to Carter's. They would point to the legal requirement restricting US loan guarantees to activities within the geographic area 'subject to Israeli administration before June 5, 1967'.

The intention behind this was to reduce the amount Israel could raise in loans from foreign banks, thus avoiding the implication that the US was helping to fund activities with which it disagreed. Mostly, the law was invoked in a half-hearted way. In late 2003, for example, the Bush administration announced that it had deducted $290 million from its loan guarantees to underscore its concerns about the route of Israel's security wall and the 'substantial amounts being spent on settlement activity'. This may seem a sizeable amount. But it was $290 million in a loan-guarantee package of $9 billion, or about 3 per cent of the total. Meanwhile, Israel was spending an estimated $560 million a year on the settlements, not including the cost of military protection, estimated at around another US$500 million a year.[2]

The strictures of US law have had little impact on settlement activity. Whatever the occasional ructions, Israeli governments of varying ideological hue pressed ahead, safe in the knowledge that domestic and international considerations meant that the US could not, and would not, walk away. If the US was an elephant on the world stage, Israel was the crafty mahout, knowing exactly which part of the beast to prod to get the right result. Eventually, the US would reward Israel's stubborn bad behaviour by declaring that the 'realities on the ground and in the region' meant that Israel could hang on to major West Bank settlements in any future deal with the Palestinians. Endorsing Ariel Sharon's proposed unilateral withdrawal of the Gaza settlements plus several small settlements in the West Bank — with a population of around 500, or about 0.2 per cent of the total West Bank settler community — President Bush declared Sharon's intention as 'historic and courageous'. The words 'long overdue and woefully inadequate' would have been more apt.

If Israel, over the years, took little notice of American strictures, it paid even less heed to international law. The Fourth Geneva Convention on the Rules of War adopted in 1949 stated: 'The occupying power cannot proceed with a transfer of one part of its own civil population into the territory occupied by it'.

One does not have to be an international lawyer to conclude that this might have posed a complication for settlement activity. During the Six Day War, Israel occupied East Jerusalem and the West Bank, the Gaza Strip, the Golan Heights, and the Sinai Peninsula. Almost immediately it gave the green light to the establishment of civilian settlements in these areas, particularly East Jerusalem.

Some four decades later (with the exception of the Sinai) the settlements had grown dramatically to accommodate nearly half a million people: East Jerusalem, 200,000; the West Bank, 230,000; the Golan Heights, 20,000; and the Gaza Strip, 7,500. Two hundred thousand-plus settlers in the West Bank against a Palestinian population of more than two million sharply underlined Drobless' fiction of the 'minority'.

The presence of the settlers was actively encouraged and funded by successive Israeli governments. But, no, these governments proclaimed, we are not in breach of international law. It does not apply to us. We captured these territories in a defensive war fought against countries that had occupied them illegally since 1948. In effect, Israel claimed the role of a successor-state, 'liberating' East Jerusalem, the West Bank, the Gaza Strip, and the Golan Heights respectively from Jordanian, Egyptian, and Syrian rule. Aronson has commented that even prime minister Eshkol, 'usually counted among the more dovish of Israel's leaders', refused to consider the West Bank as sovereign Arab territory. It had been under Jordanian occupation, held 'not by right but by force'. Israel, therefore, had merely reclaimed 'that which belonged to it'.

The sophistry was not confined to the workings of international law. Menachem Begin once explained to the Knesset's foreign affairs and defence committee that the government's policy was not to expropriate land. This would have involved an official transfer of title. Seizure was a much neater solution. It permitted the Arab owner to keep the formal title while giving exclusive possession to the government. So, wrote Aronson, Palestinian landowners 'found themselves holding worthless scraps of paper while new Jewish homes and cities arose on their lands'. To this hypocrisy we might add the imaginative claim touted by some settlement advocates that, as settlers had moved voluntarily to the territories, no 'transfer' could possibly have taken place.

Many countries, of course, pick and choose which parts of international law apply to them. Israel is by no means unusual in preferring 'facts on the ground' to the niceties of international behaviour. So leave legality aside and focus on practicality. Has the Jewish state been made more secure through its colonisation of territories occupied since 1967? Are Israelis safer because of the presence of nearly half a million of their fellow citizens in these territories?

Today, Jerusalem is firmly entrenched in Israeli hands through the ring of settlements constructed on its outskirts and those dotting East Jerusalem. The 'transfer' of civilians to these settlements has gone hand-in-hand with active discouragement of the Palestinian presence in East Jerusalem. If ever Israelis and Palestinians again talk seriously about a resolution of their conflict, this 'fact' will be exceedingly hard to unmake. But has

Israel's tight grip on Jerusalem made Jerusalemites more secure? Has it made them more relaxed about catching a bus or chatting with friends in a restaurant? Has the physical presence of Israeli settlements in East Jerusalem, in the West Bank, and in the Gaza Strip not stirred the disillusionment, bitterness and anger on which Palestinian extremism and violence has richly feasted?

'In Judea and Samaria', Drobless wrote in 1980, 'everything will be mainly determined by the facts we establish ... and less by any other considerations.' Settlements, so this argument ran, would make Israel more secure, more fulfilled. It was as though the Palestinians — ejected in 1948, conquered in 1967 — would simply roll over. It was as though Israelis believed that their nationalist urges were somehow unique. Settlements might have delayed the timeline for Palestinian statehood and greatly complicated it, but they have not made Israelis safer; in fact, just the opposite. The hundreds of thousands on the 'front line' clearly are a lot less secure. They have chosen to be here, however, and the hapless soldiers protecting them are stuck with the task.

But more than any other factor, settlements, and what they say about Israel's mentality, help explain why Palestinian bitterness and violence has flowed across the 'Green Line' (the 1967 border) into Israel proper; why ordinary Israelis visiting a café in Tel Aviv or celebrating a bar mitzvah in Haifa risk being dismembered; why grotesque images of a last bus ride in Jerusalem can lead the evening news. Settlements gave Palestinians a tangible reason to go on hating and attacking Israelis. And they undermined the standing of those on the Palestinian side who might have believed in a peaceful resolution to the conflict. Amos Elon has written that, with few exceptions, settlements

made Israel less secure. They have greatly expanded the country's lines of defence. They impose a crushing burden of protecting widely dispersed settlements deep inside densely populated Palestinian territories, where ever larger numbers of Palestinians are increasingly infuriated by the inevitable controls, curfews and violence, as well as the humiliation imposed upon them.

Even in times of relative calm, few Israelis travelled to the West Bank and the Gaza Strip. They were regarded as potentially hazardous places for anyone readily identifiable — for example, through car number plates, dress, or language — as Jewish. The inhabitants were not to be trusted. Better then to turn one's back, ignore the occupation, and get on with life inside Green Line Israel.

Such wariness was understandable. It was also a great pity. For more first-hand experience of the territories may have helped to bring home the menace of settlement policy, the physical and psychological impact of settlement building on Palestinian life and mentality. West Bank settlements often sit astride the hilltops, visible from afar. Palestinians, working and living in the valleys below, cannot but be reminded daily of the alienation of their land and their precious water resources, of the brooding, controlling presence of the Jewish state in their lives.[3]

In the Gaza Strip, around a quarter of the best agricultural land was alienated for the benefit of some 7,500 Jewish citizens of the state of Israel. Outside the barbed wire and security barriers in the West Bank, the settlers are watched by some two million Palestinians. In Gaza, another million-plus look on. 'You hate us', the Israelis complain, seemingly oblivious to the fact that settlement policy over four decades has fed that hatred. In December 1988, prime minister Yitzhak Shamir lamented to his cabinet that the 'whole world wants us to withdraw from Judea and Samaria'. The world, he said, concentrated 'more on Israeli withdrawal than on the need for peace' — as though there could be peace without withdrawal and without an end to settlements. Shamir just didn't get it.

More recently, a few wiser heads have. Take these extraordinary comments from the Labour Party MP, Avraham Burg, speaker of the Israeli parliament from 1999 to 2003:

> It is very comfortable to be a Zionist in West Bank settlements such as Beit El and Ofra. The biblical landscape is charming. From the window you can gaze through the geraniums and bougainvilleas and not see the occupation. Traveling on the fast highway takes you from Ramot on Jerusalem's northern edge to Gilo on the southern edge, a 12-minute trip that skirts barely a half-mile west of the Palestinian roadblocks, it's hard to comprehend the humiliating experience of the despised Arab who must creep for hours along the pocked, blockaded roads assigned to him. One road for the occupier, another for the occupied.

Burg, like Michael Ben-Yair and a few others, have understood the cost of occupation — to Israelis and Palestinians alike —

and the need for Israelis and Palestinians to get out of each other's lives. Yet what is truly confounding is the fact that peace-making, even when it had substance, brought little respite to settlement construction. If anything, it seemed to harden Israeli resolve that settlements were a prophylactic against Palestinian statehood.

Drobless had written in 1980 that Israel was engaged in a 'race against time'. The more facts-on-the-ground, the better Israel's capacity to define the limits of Palestinian life. In 1977, when Egyptian president Anwar Sadat made history by visiting Jerusalem, there were around 7,000 settlers in the West Bank and Gaza (plus another 50,000 in East Jerusalem). With the 1978 Camp David Accords holding out the unwelcome prospect of Palestinian autonomy, Sharon moved to reinforce that settlement beachhead. It had taken ten years for the first 5,000 settlers to arrive in the West Bank. Over the next five years another 20,000 made it — an eight-fold annual increase.

Sharon may have been the driving force behind this but the Labour Party, too, remained addicted to circumscribing the Palestinian political future. In 1993, the year that Yitzhak Rabin and Yasser Arafat shook hands on the White House lawn and the 'Oslo' peace process brought a surge of optimism, there were 116,400 settlers in the West Bank and the Gaza Strip, or 2 per cent of the total Israeli population.

While Oslo did not expressly forbid settlement expansion, it called for the 'integrity and status' of the West Bank and Gaza to be preserved in the period leading up to final status negotiations. The two sides had very different ideas what that meant.

By 1995, the year a fanatical Jewish opponent of any deal with the Palestinians shot Rabin dead, marking the beginning of the end for Oslo, settler numbers in the West Bank had grown to 134,200. Over the next five years they would climb to 198,200 or 3.1 per cent of the total Israeli population. These figures, it should be noted, are not the work of anti-Semites or Palestinian extremists — unless they inhabit Israel's Central Bureau of Statistics. For that is the source of this data.

In the ten-year period after Oslo was launched the number of Jewish settlers in the West Bank *doubled*. And not one settler departed from Gaza at official behest, despite a growing recognition within Israel that the country would be better off without entanglement in that congested and troublesome territory. Gaza would surely have been easy to give up in 1993. How hard would it have been to relocate and absorb its 7,000 settlers when Israel had taken in nearly a million Jews as the Soviet empire crumbled? How hard would it have been to insist that this sacrifice by a tiny proportion of Israel's population would be to the benefit of all? How much would the national fabric have been rent by the resort, if essential, to the tools used daily against the Palestinians — physical ejection, tear gas, bulldozers, even 'rubber bullets'?

The Gaza settlers stayed not because it made sense, not because it served any overriding theological, economic, or security purpose. They stayed because to withdraw them might have seemed like a concession, an unthinkable prospect in Israeli-Palestinian dealings. Worse, it might have implied that the settlements were wrong in the first place.

Shlomo Gazit, who had the unenviable task of running the civil administration in the territories in the first six years of occupation, has written that Israeli policy 'had one central goal: to delay for as long as possible the escalation process that would encourage extremism and lead to the outbreak of an uprising and acts of violence'. The critical word here is delay. It beggars belief that Israel imagined it could make a peace that would help to ensure its own livelihood, while working steadily and consistently to undermine its possible 'peace partner'. Yet Israel apparently believed that the Palestinians would come to the negotiation table while, almost every day, they saw more of the one-fifth of Palestine that might have been their state consumed by settlements.

What should surprise about the last decade of the twentieth century is not that there was a failed peace process. What should surprise is that there was one at all. To clothe settlement policy in the language of obfuscation — to speak of the 'natural' growth or 'thickening' of settlements — suggests that the Palestinians were idiots. Worse, the relentless drive for new and expanded settlements began to change the underlying dynamic of the conflict from a nationalist to a religious one. Anyone who argues that this will serve the security of the Jewish state is seriously deluded. No wonder Gazit called his book *Trapped Fools*.

That the settlements were ill thought out is partly explicable by the 'what do we do now' euphoria triggered by the events of 1967. Israel suddenly was geographically 20 per cent larger — and that without the Sinai or the Golan Heights. But to stick with settlements, and then to pretend that the problems of peacemaking were all of the other side's making, was farcical. Worse, it was destructively hypocritical. And, over time, it fed a mentality in some settler quarters that threatened Israel's generally proud democratic credentials.

Amos Elon has written that the settlers and their right-wing and religiously Orthodox supporters within Israel proper now control at least half the national vote. 'At their core is a group of fanatical nationalists and religious fundamentalists who believe they know exactly what God and Abraham said to each other in the Bronze Age.' An exaggeration? Perhaps. Recall, though, that Rabin was killed by two dum dum bullets fired into his back by a young Jew determined to protect this claimed legacy. At the time, there were, according to Rabin's own pollster, at least 800 other Israeli Jews prepared to do the job. Rabin, seemingly unable to comprehend the thought that one Jew might kill another, kept the poll quiet.

Consider, too, these words by a settler from the Gaza Strip, responding to Ariel Sharon's mooted evacuation of Gaza settlers: 'Whoever harms the Land of Israel ceases to be Prime Minister ... Yitzhak Rabin, to our regret was murdered. But he ceased being Prime Minister.' And note that the crudest of racial stereotypes of the Jews is returned in kind. 'Arabs are like donkeys', declared another Gaza settler, adding, with Afrikaneresque panache, 'you have to beat them all the time.'

Settlement policy has been a disaster for Israel. It brought out the worst — mentally and physically — in both Israelis and Palestinians. It brought insecurity for Israelis and despair for Palestinians. It allowed both sides to show precisely what they thought of the other and about the prospect of them living peacefully as neighbours. Settlements killed Palestinian hopes and, in turn, Palestinians killed Israelis. That is not a statement of moral equivalence. It is a statement of fact.

CHAPTER FOUR

Blood ... talk ... blood

In the early years of settlement, frictions between Zionists and the Palestinians had a decidedly everyday quality. 'We decided ... to travel to Jaffa and to try to persuade the authorities to punish the residents [of the Arab village of Aqir] for openly and with a high hand stealing the branches of our vineyards and for sending their livestock into our vineyards', recorded the 6 February 1898 minutes of the executive commit-tee of Rehovet. The Israeli historian Yaacov Ro'i, who examined the settlement's early records, wrote that in the 24 years between its founding and the outbreak of the First World War, by which time Rehovet had become the third-largest Jewish village in Palestine, 'there were a number of conflicts — some trivial, oth-ers of considerable import ... Sometimes these disputes involved entire villages ... at other times individual Arabs'. Rehovet's founders, he added, had contacts with Arabs on many levels, and 'were singularly ill-prepared for them'.

Complaints about straying animals and petty agricultural theft are, of course, a long way from today's murderous conflict. But they go to its heart. Zionism impacted profoundly on the connection between Palestinians and land they saw as theirs to

work. It made little difference if land was purchased legally for
Jewish settlements, often from urban-based Palestinian noble-
men. The result for poor tenant farmers was the same — dispossession. Palestinian resentment reflected a growing consciousness
that the demography and ownership of Palestine was inexorably
changing and should be resisted, violently if necessary.

And there was, inevitably, the growth of a semantic conflict
as well as a physical one. The violence of the other side was 'terrorism'; one's own was legitimate 'self-defence': both positions
often resting on a bedrock of hypocrisy. Both Jew and
Palestinian employed terrorism in pursuit of their political
goals. Prominent figures on each side — from future Israeli
prime ministers Menachem Begin and Yitzhak Shamir, to the
Grand Mufti of Jerusalem, Hajj Amin al-Husseini, and the shop-
worn Yasser Arafat — keenly understood the strategic value of
unpredictable, indiscriminate violence.

Mass killings became historical bookmarks, fuelling both
commemoration and the hunger for revenge: the 1929 slaugh-
ter of Jews in Hebron; the planting of a mine in a Haifa market
in 1938 by Begin's Etzel (Irgun) movement which killed more
than 70 Palestinians; the catalogue of Palestinian attacks against
Jewish men, women and children; the massacre of Palestinians
in Beirut in 1982, under Israel's indifferent gaze; the brutal,
deafening destruction of ordinary Israelis at the hands of
Palestinian suicide bombers. The list of places and victims is
seemingly endless.

Menachem Begin publicly acknowledged the usefulness of
the 'legend of terror' that he had helped create at Deir Yassin in

1948. Others were less impressed. Later that year as he visited America, a letter in *The New York Times* described his 'Freedom Party' as terrorist, chauvinist and 'closely akin in its organis-ation, methods, political philosophy and social appeal to the Nazi and Fascist parties'. Among the letter's signatories were Albert Einstein and Hannah Arendt.

In *Trapped Fools*, Shlomo Gazit noted that after Israel's occupation of the West Bank in 1967 the signs of Palestinian resistance 'came very early', with the first 'terrorist attacks' beginning in August that year. From that moment, 'the terri-tories were never calm'. He wrote that it was

> curious that the leaders of the violent Jewish revolt in Palestine — Menachem Begin and his friends ... as well as Yitzhak Shamir and his friends in Lehi, who fought mightily against the [British] 'foreign occupier' — of all people, could not understand that the Palestinians would study Zionist history voraciously and learn the lessons of the Jewish underground movements.

Palestinian extremists had several role models to choose from. In *Religious Fundamentalism and Political Extremism*, Arie Perlinger from Haifa University and Leonard Weinberg, professor of political science at Nevada University, wrote that 'Etzel's world view ... considered political violence and terrorism legitimate tools in the Jewish national struggle for the land of Israel'. But Etzel, they observed, 'was neither the most violent nor the most extreme Jewish nationalist group ... Moreover, it was not this group that laid the foundations for

Jewish terrorism following statehood. This role is reserved for
the Lehi organization', first led by Yair Stern and later by Yitzhak
Shamir, a future Israeli prime minister.

Perlinger and Weinberg commented that, more than any other
Jewish group, the Lehi 'considered a violent struggle in general,
and terrorism in specific, to be legitimate measures for realising
... national liberation ... to inflict real harm ... while simultane-
ously calling the world's attention to the struggle of the Jewish
people'. Among Lehi's victims were Lord Moyne, the British 'resident minister' for the Middle East, assassinated in Cairo in late
1944; and the visiting UN representative, Swedish Count Folke
Bernadotte, assassinated in Jerusalem in September 1948.

How easy a transition it was from Jewish to Palestinian violence in the name of 'national liberation'. A 1980 study by Hanan
Alon, conducted under the auspices of the Rand Corporation,
divided Palestinian violence against the Jews into three phases:

- 1919–1948: terrorism inflicted by local Arab groups
  against the growing Jewish population in British-
  controlled Palestine. This, said Alon, 'was motivated
  mainly by the goal to deny the Zionists political aspirations, rather than to promote Palestinian national goals'.
- 1949–1956: terrorist acts along the 1948 armistice lines,
  inflicted by fedayin groups infiltrating from the West
  Bank (then under Jordanian control) and the Gaza Strip
  (under Egyptian control). Again, Alon argued, that 'no
  particular Palestinian national aspirations and goals were
  involved'.

- 1965–onwards: terrorism that was carried out by a number of Palestinian groups as part of the armed struggle aimed at 'liberating Palestine' and establishing a Palestinian state which would replace Israel and also include the West Bank and the Gaza Strip.

The accuracy of Alon's timeline for the growth of Palestinian political consciousness is debatable. The denial of 'Zionist political aspirations' certainly suggests that other aspirations were at work. After all, the 1937 Peel Report had commented that the 'underlying causes' of the disturbances in 1936 involved the 'desire of the Arabs for national independence' combined with 'their hatred and fear of the establishment of the Jewish National Home'. The report added that these 'two causes were the same as those of all the previous outbreaks and have always been inextricably linked together'.

But leaving aside the timeline for Palestinian national awakening, the 1967 Six Day War gave Palestinian violence new impetus. All Palestinians in the 22 per cent of the country not part of the Jewish state after 1948 were now under Israeli occupation. This occupation quickly led to settlement activity. That this in turn led to violence should have surprised no-one.

Geoffrey Aronson described three stages in Palestinian reactions after 1967. He characterised these as: rejection, when Palestinian opposition to Israeli occupation was 'a constant feature'; depression, when 'the risks of opposing occupation were always greater than acquiescing in it'; and, eventually, a 'renewal of faith', after the emergence of the Palestinian Liberation

Organization as the 'sole, legitimate representative of the
Palestinian people'. The PLO, founded by the Arab states in
1964, and energised after its takeover by Yasser Arafat and his
Fatah movement in 1969,[1] became, in Aronson's words, 'the
only credible counterweight to a constellation of powers —
Israeli, American and Arab — each with its own self-interested
solution to the Palestinian problem'.

Alon argued that the reasons for the increase in Palestinian
violence after the Six Day War included:

- A realisation that regular Arab forces could not win a war
  against Israel. Terrorism provided a means of keeping the
  conflict going while these forces were rebuilt.
- Palestinians under Israeli occupation in Gaza and the
  West Bank gave 'new content to the notion of a "War of
  liberation" ' and new opportunity to mobilise the masses
  for an insurgency. A Fatah manifesto distributed in the
  Gaza Strip and the West Bank in September 1967 called
  for a war of liberation, exhorted Palestinians standing
  close to Israeli cars 'to fill the gas tank with sand or sugar,'
  and included advice on making petrol bombs.[2]
- A proliferation of Palestinian terrorist organizations, in
  part competing against one another to justify their existence. According to Alon, over 72 per cent of the almost
  7,000 terrorist operations carried out between June 1967
  and December 1978 occurred in the first three years.
  However, the failure of the 'Vietnamisation' of the Israeli-
  Palestinian conflict, the increasing effectiveness of Israeli

countermeasures, and the lack of impact of the operations, led militant Palestinian organizations to open a new front — international terrorism, most conspicuously against planes and airports. The proportion of such strikes was tiny (less than 3 per cent), but they served a keen purpose in putting the Palestinian issue 'on the international agenda'.

A question posed by Alon bears careful thinking about today. Between 1967 and 1978 a total of 9,424 Israeli civilians lost their lives through misadventure. Of these, 6,312 or 66.9 per cent died in car accidents. This compared to 19.6 per cent in labour accidents and 10.6 per cent through criminal violence. The figure for terrorism was 272 deaths, or a mere 2.9 per cent of the total. Why, Alon asked, do societies perceive terrorism

as a 'new threat', more serious than other hazards they face? Why do people seem to tolerate casualties inflicted by terrorism much less than those generated by other causes? Why do governments share this attitude towards terrorism?

Alon's answer underlined the effectiveness of terrorism as a weapon — its indiscriminate, unpredictable quality, preferably 'with many victims'. People were 'fascinated by large incidents'. What counted was 'the number of casualties per incident and not aggregate casualty statistics'. Every Israeli would 'remember the 24 school children killed and the 62 wounded by three terrorists in Ma'alot in northern Israel on 15 May, 1974; or the takeover of two buses on the coastal highway on March 11, 1978, when 33 passengers were killed and 82 wounded'. Media publicity was a critical element in determining the 'success' of an operation, with one of the great terrorist fears that of 'being ignored'. On this, the American author Don DeLillo has observed that terrorism is 'the language of being noticed'.

The same year that Alon's study was published, the Israeli historian Professor Jacob Talmon wrote an open letter to prime minister Begin calling for an end to Israel's policies of occupation and settlement. Talmon stated prophetically: 'The combination of subjection, national oppression and social inferiority is a time bomb ... Let us not compel the Arabs to feel that they have been humiliated until they believe that hope is gone and they must die for Palestine.'

His appeal fell on deaf ears. Violence and its handmaiden — publicity — would continue as a way of life, and death, for Palestinians. The factors driving this, Palestinian resentment of the Israeli presence in the West Bank and the Gaza Strip, and the denial by some Palestinians of Israel's right to exist, are now more deeply entrenched than ever. Political leaders, the media, and others have rightly decried the deliberately mass and indiscriminate nature of much Palestinian violence and the attendant vicious 'cycle of violence'.

This cycle has become a road-without-end, every action demanding a vengeful reaction. In early 1996, for example, in a clever intelligence operation, Israel blew off the head of Hamas' chief bomb-maker, Yahya Ayyash ('the Engineer'), using a mobile phone. Hamas took its revenge on Israeli bus commuters a few weeks later.[3] In early 2004, Israel assassinated the two leading Hamas figures Sheikh Ahmed Yassin and Dr Abdel Aziz al-Rantisi. In doing so it removed two strident critics of the Jewish state. Such actions may well have bought time for the future victims of Hamas attacks. But they will not guarantee them peace of mind or an old-age pension.

After Yassin's assassination, the senior Israeli journalist Nahum Barnea wrote that 'Sheikh Yassin bears responsibility for the death of hundreds of Jews in his life. The question that ought to trouble us now is how many Jews he will kill in his death.' The Israeli opposition leader, Shimon Peres, no stranger to 'targeted assassinations' — he had ordered Ayyash's killing — described Yassin's murder as 'poor judgement'. In typically high-minded fashion, he added that 'only by assassinating the reasons for terror can we assassinate terror'.

No figure on the Palestinian side has embodied more tellingly the contradictions between 'terrorist' and 'freedom fighter', between flexibility and duplicity, between the pragmatic and the dogmatic, or between survival and leadership abilities, than Yasser Arafat. Arafat long recognised the strategic value of terrorism, declaring to the Western media in 1968:

Israel is not just an army. It is a society that can only survive and prosper on peace and security. We aim to disrupt that society. Insecurity will make a mess of their agriculture and commerce. It will halt immigration and encourage migration. We will disrupt their tourist industry.

Under Arafat, Fatah, which he and a handful of close

comrades had founded in the late 1950s, became the strongest of the various Palestinian armed organizations. In 1969, Arafat became chairman of the PLO, taking over from Yahya Hamuda who had acted in the position after Ahmed Shukeiry had been forced to resign, purportedly for his 'opposition to commando activities against Israel'. With its leader now heading the overall resistance movement, Fatah wasted no time. In 1969 it carried out some 2,500 attacks on Israeli targets. According to the historian Walter Lacquer, what distinguished Fatah from the other Palestinian groups was its sheer size, the extent of its funding (much of it from the Arab oil states), and the political support it enjoyed internationally.

In 1974, wearing his trademark black-and-white keffiya (headscarf) carefully crafted in the shape of (all of) Palestine, Arafat told the United Nations General Assembly, 'I am a rebel and freedom is my cause ... I have come bearing an olive branch and a freedom fighter's gun.[4] Do not let the olive branch fall from my hand.' That same year, Edgar O'Balance, in *Arab Guerilla Power*, offered this portrait of the PLO leader:

Arafat is an astute politician forever angling for more power, rather than a wise statesman planning for a sound future ... his military capabilities are considerably less than his political gifts ... Arafat was overwhelmed by his own verbosity ... he became deeply immersed in his own personality cult ... In many ways he falls short of being a great leader. An advocate of power without responsibility, he sought to use governments while striving to remain independent of them.

Thirty years later, Arafat's biographers were still trying to get his measure. One of them, the Israeli academic Barry Rubin, argued that no one in the world was 'a more thoroughgoing exemplar' of politics-as-theatre:

> Arafat was ... always on stage, doing a different part in each scene, and starring in a new play every few weeks. To the Western audience, he would often play Charlie Chaplin, the pitiful, home-less yet loveable outcast; to the Arab or Islamic audience, he would act the part of Salah al-Din.

One of the most important scenes in which Arafat played, and which would critically shape the history of the Israeli-Palestinian conflict in the early years of the twenty-first century, was acted out in July 2000 at Camp David. There, president Clinton, keen to put the memory of Monica Lewinsky's under-garments behind him, and with an eye on his place in history, strove to bring Israelis and Palestinians to accord. The meeting broke up in confusion and recrimination with the Israeli prime minister, Ehud Barak, going on to declare that there was no one to talk to on the Palestinian side. Fierce criticism was directed at Arafat for his rejection of Barak's purportedly 'generous' offer, said to involve Palestinian control of most of the West Bank and shared authority in key parts of East Jerusalem. It became an article of faith among Arafat's detractors that his obduracy at Camp David finally ended the peace hopes of the 1990s, trig-gered the Palestinian uprising a couple of months later, and plunged the region into new despair.

Nonetheless, even trenchant Arafat critics, such as Rubin, observed that during the Camp David meeting 'nothing was written'. At Barak's insistence, every idea was left in the ether. The participants' comprehension of what was on offer, and what was not, depended on their listening abilities. Anyone who has ever had a conversation, let alone been involved in a negotiation, will know the hazards in later getting an agreed version of what was said — especially if the issues are as contentious as they were, and are, between Israelis and Palestinians. Yet that was the story of Camp David.

According to Rubin, with little direct part to play in the negotiations, Arafat was stuck in his cabin all day. 'Like a caged animal, he paced furiously back and forth.' This less-than-human view of the PLO leader, it might be noted, fits neatly with an earlier characterisation of Palestinians as 'drugged cockroaches in a bottle' by the Israeli chief of staff, Rafael Eitan. After the failure of Camp David even Ehud Barak got into the animal imagery, commenting that maybe 'the Palestinians are like crocodiles — the more you give them, the more they want'.

A more nuanced view of Camp David came from another Israeli author, David Horovitz, editor of the fortnightly magazine, *Jerusalem Report*. In his *Still Life with Bombers: Israel in the Age of Terrorism*, Horovitz described Camp David as 'the cracked foundation stone on which everything crumbled so completely in the subsequent years'. The great difficulty, he wrote, was that there was no independent, unarguable account of what went on, who said what, and how it fell apart.

There was no silent American factotum sitting in the corner writing a protocol; that was at Barak's insistence. If they reached a deal, it would be drafted and signed, and the festivities would begin. But if they did not ... he [Barak] did not want to leave Arafat in a position to cite chapter and verse on what Israel had been prepared to relinquish, and use the protocols as the starting point for the next round of negotiations.

It was this approach, said Horovitz, that produced what he termed the battle of the narratives: 'the Israeli versions, the Palestinian versions and the American versions', with dissensions and contradictions within each delegation, 'most starkly among the Americans'. Still, in keeping with the dominant 'narrative' of Camp David, Horovitz blamed Arafat for its failure, and by extension the demise of the Oslo process. The Camp David meeting, said Horovitz, did not collapse over 'what Palestinian spin doctors have since presented as the key obstacle: the occupation. Barak went to Camp David determined to end the occupation. Arafat wouldn't let him.'

If only it were that clear-cut, that *knowable*. A former US ambassador to Israel, Martin Indyk, suggested after Camp David that there was plenty of blame to go round. Arafat had no reason to trust Barak who, after all, had turned his considerable energies to the Palestinian issue only when his peace overtures to Syria over the Golan Heights had been rebuffed. Arafat was expected to fit into Barak's new schedule and an American president's valedictory. And as much as anyone else he would have been keenly aware of the wreckage of broken promises —

written as well as unwritten — that littered the history of Israeli-Palestinian dealings, not all of them of Palestinian making.

Amos Elon has commented that Barak's purported 'unprecedented generosity' at Camp David, when it came to Jerusalem, 'did not go beyond offering the Palestinians sovereignty over a few isolated Palestinian enclaves cut off from the Palestinian state and from one another by ... new Israeli neighbourhoods'. Barak offered the Palestinians 'sovereignty over their mosques ... but not over the ground on which they stood'.

If nothing else, Barak's grand failing was that of naivety. He approached Camp David like the impatient ex-general he was. By Israeli standards he may have been in a magnanimous frame of mind. He was certainly generous to Israeli settlers in East Jerusalem — not one of whom would have had to move — and to West Bank settlers — most of whom could have stayed where they were. Barak's own words since suggest that the deal floated at Camp David was not quite as straightforward as some would like to believe. In August 2003, he wrote in the Israeli daily newspaper, *Yedi'ot Aharonot*:

Here's the truth: Barak did not give away a thing. I made clear and I am proud of it, that in exchange for an end to the conflict and giving up the right of [Palestinian refugee] return, 80 per cent of the settlers under Israeli sovereignty, recognition of the security needs of Israel and of Israel's affinity to the holy places, we will be ready for painful, defined concessions that lead to a Palestinian state.

Arafat alone was not responsible for the collapse of Camp David. That said, his was a profound failure — that of will. He simply could not bring himself to test Israeli positions; he would not take a chance. For all his durability and craftiness, nothing will now change his dismal legacy to the Palestinian people. For all the millions of words that have been written since, O'Balance's pen-portrait of Arafat — a man consumed by his own image — has stood the test of time. After September 2000, when Arafat's bête noire, Ariel Sharon, helped light the fuse for the second Palestinian intifada (uprising), the question was sharpened whether, in spite of his purportedly splintered, enigmatic personality, Arafat was, in fact, a one-dimensional leader unable to make the critical transition. A man with a singular capacity to feed his critics' fears that, whatever the makeovers, he had never given up on the dream of a chaotic end to Israel: poacher turned gamekeeper, but always with a glint in his eye about the 'good old days'. Arafat saw himself as the new Saladin, driving the 'infidels' from Jerusalem.

He ended up sounding increasingly like Hajj Amin al-Husseini, whose implacable opposition to compromise, any compromise, and his supping with the Nazis during World War II, so damaged the Palestinian cause. Corrupt and dictatorial, Arafat believed he could end an historical injustice by sitting tight — epitomising the Palestinian conviction that the scales of justice inevitably would tilt their way, almost by divine intervention. He should have known better about God's little tricks in the Middle East. In *How Israel Lost* the Pulitzer prize-winning American author Richard Ben Kramer argued that Arafat was recalled to Palestine 'to give his people a state of their own and a government that was for them'. Instead, he attended 'only to his own power and perquisites, which he considers the same thing as government'.

In a detailed 2002 report on Palestinian suicide bombing, bearing the eerily appropriate title, *Erased in a Moment*, Human Rights Watch commented that the 'greatest failure' of Arafat and his Palestinian Authority (PA) 'for which they must bear heavy responsibility' was their 'unwillingness to deploy the criminal justice system decisively' against Palestinian extremists. There is much truth in this claim. Arafat lived in a world where account-ability simply did not matter. The PLO had long believed in a combined military and political struggle. When Arafat addressed the UN in 1974 he had checked his gun at the door. Two decades later, even at the height of the Oslo peacemaking process, it was close at hand. And, when the new century dawned, and Israelis and Palestinians rediscovered their taste for killing each other, Arafat's inability to eschew violence — demonstrably and unequivocally — was once more on display.

Ironically, the Israelis helped to provide him with the excuses and rationale for his inaction in dealing with Palestinian violence. In what *The Economist* described as 'state-building in reverse' Israel, under Sharon, destroyed Arafat's security assets while demanding that he impose national authority. As it did so, the Palestinian academic Khalil Shikaki wrote that if Arafat successfully suppressed his internal opponents he risked 'being seen ... as an Israeli lackey'; if unsuccessful, he faced 'a civil war'. And so, as he was wont to do, Arafat dithered and eventually was hung out to dry by Israel and the US administration. As though, somehow, that would fix the problem. As though the blockage was little more than that of Arafat's opaque personality and troublesome sense of commitment.

The first Palestinian intifada, which erupted in 1987 and petered out in the early 1990s, left more than 1,400 Palestinians and 300 Israelis dead. It also left an important political legacy, convincing many Israelis that they had to find a way of ending the occupation of the Gaza Strip and much of the West Bank. The intifada was a victory for Palestinian street-power. It led, at least indirectly, to the peace efforts of the 1990s and the gradual hand-over of land and authority to the Palestinians under Arafat, who made a victorious entry into Gaza in mid-1994.

The second intifada broke out in the wake of the failed Camp David meeting, the ostensible trigger being the then opposition leader Ariel Sharon's provocative tour of the Temple Mount complex in Jerusalem's Old City. Amos Elon has rightly described the complex, known to Muslims as the Haram al-Sharif (Noble Sanctuary) and the third-holiest site in Islam, as 'Jerusalem's most contentious piece of real estate'. Sharon's action was driven by domestic political considerations — a determination to thwart Benjamin Netanyahu's political come-back. It worked, and Sharon ended up prime minister. That does not make him single-handedly responsible for the violence of the past few years. It does make him culpable. He, with Arafat, presided over a descent into the abyss which, in less than four years, killed some four thousand people and injured many more, the bulk of them Palestinian.

The hopes of the mid-1990s evaporated; perhaps, in fact, they were an aberration. Perhaps the real measure of how Israelis and Palestinians see each other is best symbolised by the attack helicopter and the suicide bomber. When Israel regrets the 'by-catch' of Palestinians killed or injured in operations against Palestinian militants, or alleged militants, there is a predictable, cynical response among Palestinians. When Arafat condemns terrorist attacks, but does little or nothing to counteract the image of suicide bombers as 'martyrs', and even provides financial succour for some of those involved, Israeli cynicism about his motives is rightly strengthened.[5] When senior Palestinian Authority figures speak, as they have done, of suicide bombings as 'the normal response ... for all the Israelis have done in the refugee camps, to Palestinian civilians, women and children', there seems no way out. History and the Israeli occupation do not justify Palestinian terrorism; but, in turn, terrorism does not justify occupation and some Israeli behaviour. The seemingly inseparable Siamese twins of Israeli and Palestinian violence have poisoned both peoples.

Palestinians did not invent the idea of suicide bombing. But in the early 1990s it became their weapon of choice. One of its first advocates was a co-founder of Islamic Jihad, Fathi Shikaki. In the late 1980s, he spoke openly of a strategy of 'exceptional' martyrdom, where the mujahid (struggler) would not waver or escape but 'execute a successful explosion for religion and jihad', destroying the morale of the enemy and planting 'terror into the people'. In the early 1990s, the Hamas bomb-maker Yahya Ayyash urged the organization's leadership to employ 'human bombs' to make 'the cost of the occupation ... that much more unbearable'. In Jane's *Terrorism and Security Monitor* John Daley wrote in September 2001 that suicide bombings 'are the most feared weapons in the arsenal of political activists'. He added that although some Palestinian attacks were carried out against military targets, most were aimed at civilians — a Hamas training manual noted the foolishness of hunting the tiger when there were 'plenty of sheep around'. The Human Rights Watch report tellingly described the suicide bomber's target as 'everyday life'. Few can hide from that.

Many of us can probably imagine what it must be like to take up arms to defend or advance a cause. The suicide bomber challenges our imagination in a particularly gruesome way. It is an act of random brutality specifically aimed at maximising fear and revulsion. Why one bus rather than another; why this café instead of that one; why this shopping mall? Is it merely a question of numbers or opportunity, or do other, more subjective, factors come into play? Do suicide bombers look their victims in the eye as they reach for the trigger? In a foreword to Barbara Victor's 2003 book on Palestinian female suicide bombers, *Army of Roses*, *Newsweek*'s Christopher Dickey wrote of the 'intensely personal and direct decision' required of the bomber:

> The would-be martyr stands before her victims: soldiers, sometimes, or perhaps other women just shopping for dinner, or maybe a girl very much like herself. And she pushes the button or she does not. She, and she alone decides.

Or, in the more prosaic words of one Hamas leader, with 'an explosive belt or bag, the bomber has control over vision, location, and timing'.

Bombers 'sponsored' by Hamas or Islamic Jihad have mostly cited religion as explanation and justification for their deed. But the suicide bomber's impulse originates more likely in an imprecise, heady mix of religion interwoven with the Palestinian nationalist cause and the hunger for revenge. In 1988, Arafat's Fatah movement accepted the distinction between pre-1967 Israel and the Palestinian territories of the Gaza Strip and the West Bank. This was later incorporated into the 1993 Oslo Accords. For a time Hamas, though not the less influential Islamic Jihad, also appeared to have accepted this demarcation. As late as 2003, Sheikh Yassin stated that the 'main battle has always been against Israeli soldiers and settlers'. Attacks inside Israel, he claimed, were a 'response to Israel's crimes against our people. They are not the strategy of our movement ... [which] is to defend ourselves against an occupying army and settlers and settlements'.

Just before he was assassinated by the Israelis in August 2003, the Hamas figure Abu Shanab identified the 1994 murder of 29 Palestinians at prayer in Hebron as a turning point in the organization's strategy. 'The massacre did not leave us any choice. They attacked us at our weakest point, so we had to do the same in return. We did not want this kind of struggle but were left with no choice.' Earlier, Abu Shanab had explained to an American academic the cost-effectiveness of suicide bombing. It required merely a detonator and a 'moment of courage', the latter possibly coming from having seen 'something terrible, some kind of atrocity'.

Writing in the *New York Review of Books* in January 2003, the Israeli academic Avishai Margalit examined the motives and the impact of Palestinian suicide bombers. Noting the importance of religious belief and symbolism for many of them, he suggested, nonetheless, that 'the main motivating force ... seems to be the desire for a spectacular revenge'. Vengeance through suicide bombing had the additional value of 'making yourself the victim of your own act, and thereby putting your tormentors to moral shame'. Contradicting Sheikh Yassin's later assertion that Hamas drew a clear distinction between the occupied territories and Israel proper, Margalit argued that for both Hamas and Islamic Jihad, motives of revenge were mixed, with the message

> that Islam has been divinely endowed with the entire land of Palestine, which includes all of Israel, and that this sacred endowment is not subject to negotiation. Sending suicide bombers into Israel proper rather than confining them to the occupied territories gives a clear signal that the two Islamic organizations do not accept the distinction between the pre-1967 land of Israel and the land ... conquered in 1967.

Margalit emphasised the way suicide attacks had undermined both Palestinian and Israeli society. They had devastated the Palestinian economy through closing off opportunities for Palestinian labour and products to enter the vital Israel market. And, if revenge were a principal goal, the suicide bombers had

succeeded 'in hurting Israel very badly', and not just by killing
and injuring many civilians.

> A more far-reaching success is that Israel's leaders, in retaliating,
> have behaved so harshly, putting three million people under siege,
> with recurring curfews for unlimited periods of time, all in front
> of the world press and television, with the result that Israel may
> now be the most hated country in the world. This is hugely dam-
> aging to Israel, since the difference between being hated and losing
> legitimacy is dangerously narrow … Israel claims it is fighting a
> war against the 'infrastructure of terrorism', but in fact it is
> destroying the infrastructure of the entire Palestinian society …

A year before Margalit's article appeared, Waffa Idris had
blown herself up on Jerusalem's busy Jaffa Road, killing an 81-
year-old man and injuring more than 100 people. Idris became
the 47th Palestinian, but the first woman, to strap on a bomb
belt and demonstrate that, for her, the most valuable aspect of
life was how it ended. She was also the perpetrator of the first
suicide bombing claimed by the al-Aqsa Martyrs' Brigades, affil-
iated with Fatah. However much Idris's religion blessed and
comforted this act, however much the hate in her heart drove a
hunger for revenge, it was, and remains, an act of defiant hope-
lessness. Rightly or wrongly, Palestinians see Israel as daily providing the justification for their own terrible deeds. Rightly or
wrongly, they come to value their life only for its capacity to
destroy others. How much have Israeli and Palestinian leaders
failed their peoples when, in Margalit's words, 'civilians of one

society regularly volunteer to become suicide bombers who target civilians of another society'. We might be shamed and revolted by this, but should we really be surprised? For decades, Israelis and Palestinians have debased one another and, in so doing, have debased themselves.

'Israel, having ceased to care about the children of the Palestinians', wrote Avraham Burg in 2003,

> should not be surprised when they come washed in hatred and blow themselves up in the centers of Israeli escapism. They consign themselves to Allah in our places of recreation, because their own lives are a torture. They spill their blood in our restaurants in order to ruin our appetites, because they have children and parents at home who are hungry and humiliated. We could kill a thousand ringleaders and engineers a day and nothing will be solved, because the leaders come up from below — from the wells of hatred and anger, from the 'infrastructures' of injustice and moral corruption.

Occupation, violence, and terror have produced a paralysing mind-set. Israel argues that as long as there is violence there will be occupation. Palestinians counter that as long as there is occupation there will be violence. This refrain reverberates more loudly than ever. Even during the 1990s, when peace plans lay on the table, there was little respite from violence. Israelis and Palestinians killed the other and they killed their own. Palestinian 'collaborators' paid with their lives, as did prime minister Yitzhak Rabin. Now, with the 'peace process' little more than an outsider's conceit, the motivation for Palestinians to go on killing Israelis is especially strong. Some may seek a spectacular martyrdom; others kill Jews because of who they are and where they are. They kill them because they have no good reason not to.

Consider these words penned by Gideon Levy in January 2004 for *Ha'aretz* newspaper. Israelis had 'little interest in knowing the lay of the land from which terror springs'. Few were 'capable of imagining what life is like' in the 'imprisoned villages' from where the bombers came: the 'almost universal unemployment, poverty, endless siege and humiliations of life inside a prison. A young man ... had no reason to get up in the morning other than to face another day of joblessness and humiliation'. Israel, Levy wrote, had

> counted 81 days of quiet without terrorist attack. But there is no greater lie than this. The quiet was only here. During this 'quiet' dozens of Palestinians were killed and almost no one bothered to report it. That is how it becomes possible to speak of quiet and then claim that the Palestinians disturbed it ... we count only our own dead, all the rest don't exist.

But, Levy observed, there is an Israeli price for the many concealed Palestinian dead. 'They are an incentive to terrorism. Their exclusion from our agenda cannot make the results of their killing disappear as well.'

Violence was employed in the creation of the Jewish state. It underlined the determination of some Zionists to see their cause to its 'natural' conclusion. But Israel arose from an extraordinary confluence of historical and political factors. It arose from the grotesque violence of the Holocaust, not wanton acts of terror by Jewish settlers in Palestine. Palestinian violence has kept the Palestinian issue on the world stage. From the hijacking and destruction of passenger aircraft in the 1970s to the egregious violence of the suicide bomber, the Palestinians have ensured the world will not forget them. Violence, however, has not achieved and will not achieve Palestinian political aspirations. Just as Israelis, in Burg's words, can 'kill a thousand ringleaders and engineers a day and nothing will be solved', so no amount of memorialising suicide 'martyrs' will bring a freer, more contented life for Palestinians.

Worse, violence is becoming an end in itself. Barbara Victor's *Army of Roses* offered the chilling observation that among Palestinian school children, little girls as well as little boys 'say they longed to be suicide bombers'; that a 'culture of death' has permeated Palestinian society, guaranteeing 'the destruction of future generations'.

And those generations will not just be Palestinian.

CHAPTER FIVE

Whither the Zionist enterprise?

O ne of the easiest things to find in Israel is an argument. That, undoubtedly, is one of the country's sharpest, most enduring qualities. For, however much non-Israelis become absorbed in the issues of Israel and Palestine, however conscious they may be about the ripple effect of events there on the wider world, however critical or laudatory they may be about Israeli or Palestinian behaviour, debate among Israelis themselves is unmatchable for its energy, passion and commitment. Debate ranges, and often rages, across the spectrum: from ardent believers in uncompromising Jewish control of the entire Land of Israel — whose pronouncements at times are steeped in racism — to those who would fashion a unitary state in which Jews, inevitably, would one day be a minority. Take, as an example, the mooted withdrawal of Israeli settlers from the Gaza Strip. Welcomed by many Israelis as a step to help secure their country's future, it is castigated by some others as the beginning of the end — a precedent for the 'ethnic cleansing' of Jews from anywhere.

There are good reasons for Israeli fractiousness. It reflects not just the intellectual and political vigour of the country, but also the nature of the state. For more than half a century, Israelis have been living alongside, and on top of, another people. Despite all that accumulated experience, despite the agonised soul-searching by some Israelis, and for all the casual and brutal dismissal by others of Palestinian aspirations, Israel is no nearer to resolving the fundamental dilemma of its creation: what to do with and about the Palestinians; how to be accepted as an organic part of its region and not as a twentieth-century Crusader infiltration. Israel exists, justly proud of its achievements, rightly seeing itself as being at the centre of the Jewish firmament. It may not be the 'light unto the nations' of Biblical declaration, but Jews can live a free life in Israel. The country, however, cannot free itself from the conditions of its making. No matter how much the early Zionists wished it to be true, Palestine was *never* a land without people. The making of one nationalist dream involved the unmaking of another.

And, for some lovers of Zion, that unmaking did not go far enough. The residual Palestinian presence in the State of Israel after 1948 suggested an incompleteness in the Jewish return, a tourniquet on the pulse of Zionism's fulfilment. The logical reaction then, indeed the only one, was to remove that non-Jewish presence. Long before the terminology of 'ethnic cleansing' entered popular vocabulary, the concept and the practice was alive and well in Zionist thinking, as 'transfer'. And not just at the margins — we have already touched on Herzl's idea of a 'discreet' spiriting of the 'penniless population' across the border, and Ben-Gurion's attachment to the idea of expulsion.

'Transfer', of course, was a gentler, more peaceful term, almost with implications of a trade: 'Leave, and we'll leave you alone!' And it was a neat solution. Israelis could hold on to land freed of undesirable non-Jewish inhabitants. They could redeem their historic claim. All they needed to do was to ignore the fact that the Palestinians might feel an attachment to the same land, where they had for centuries been born and raised and buried; that they might not welcome being 'relocated'; and that they might one day retaliate.

Take these two analyses of 'transfer'. The first is by the prominent 'revisionist' historian Benny Morris; the second, by a Palestinian born in the Galilee, Nur Masalha, now a British-based academic. Morris has probably done more than any other Israeli to debunk the myth that, in the face of the violence and uncertainty of 1948, the Palestinians spontaneously and conveniently decamped. Some did, it is true. Many did not — they were urged away at the point of a gun. Morris's 'revision' of this falsehood of Israel's foundation has made him both famous and notorious. Extraordinarily, he has now revised his revisionism, not resiling from his claim that the Palestinians were pushed, but concluding that they were not pushed hard enough.

According to Morris, from April 1948 Ben-Gurion was 'projecting a message of transfer'. There was no explicit order in writing, but the idea was 'in the air. The entire leadership understands that this is the idea. The officer corps understands what is required of them … a consensus of transfer is created.' And, Morris now says, Ben-Gurion was right. In certain conditions

expulsion is not a war crime. I don't think the expulsions of 1948 were war crimes … You have to dirty your hands … There are circumstances in history which justify ethnic cleansing ... A Jewish state would not have come into being without the uprooting of 700,000 Palestinians. Therefore it was necessary to uproot them ... It was necessary to cleanse the hinterland and cleanse the border areas and cleanse the main roads ... I know it doesn't sound nice but ... the need to establish this state in this place overcame the injustice that was done to the Palestinians by uprooting them ... Even the great American democracy could not have been created without the annihilation of the Indians. There are cases in which the overall, final good justifies harsh and cruel acts.

Palestinians, no doubt, will be relieved to know that the distress of being driven from their homes in 1948 was serving a noble cause. Those few American Indians whose ancestors escaped 'annihilation' will be similarly reassured. As will the Aborigines of Australia and all indigenous peoples who inconvenienced the settlement and civilising plans of those with a higher 'moral' purpose. If this is an example of the 'light unto the nations' at work it will, for many, be much safer to stay in the dark. Morris does have one complaint — that the expulsions did not go far enough, that Ben-Gurion got 'cold feet' and possibly made a 'fatal mistake' in not finishing the job. If Ben-Gurion had 'cleansed the whole country', had resolved the matter 'once and for all', Israel would now be 'quieter and know less suffering'.

That is an arguable proposition. It is equally arguable that with greater numbers of Palestinian refugees shoved into the surrounding region, Israel would have seen even less security than it has in the past fifty years. And what of the tens of thousands of Jews then still living in the Arab world? Would they have simply been shipped off to Israel, now that there was an early vacancy, with no questions asked?

In Morris's apocalyptic view the task, one day, will have to be finished. 'I am ready to tell you that in other circumstances ... which are liable to be realised in five or ten years, I see expulsions ... They may even be essential.' And it will not just target the Palestinians of the occupied territories. For the million-plus Israeli Arabs are a 'time bomb'. Their slide 'into complete Palestinization [sic] has made them an emissary of the enemy ... If the threat to Israel is existential, expulsion will be justified.'

Nur Masalha has written a book called *Land with a people: Israel, transfer and the Palestinians, 1949–1996*. While it is not an angry volume, it captures the seeds of Palestinian anger, exploring the theological, territorial and political dynamics shaping Jewish thought and action over the Palestinian 'interlopers'. The theological imperative rested on God's command to the Jews to live in the Land of Israel. Did this not make 'transfer' an inevitable part of God's work? Rabbi Shlomo Aviner declared that Arab 'possession' of the land had 'no legal and moral validity'. Rabbi Tzvi Yehuda Kook, the son of Israel's first Ashkenazi chief rabbi and the spiritual father of the settler movement, argued that the Torah prohibited 'giving up even an inch of our liberated land'. There was 'no Arab land here, only the inheritance of our God'. Kook added, hopefully, that 'the more the world gets used to this thought the better it will be for it and for all of us'.

Most of the world did not quite see it that way. But the ideologues, spiritual and otherwise, were not to be deterred. Masalha has commented that the Zionist assertion of 'historical rights' meant that Arab possession of the land was 'morally flawed and legally, at best temporary'. If Arab residency in Palestine was 'based on theft', Arab removal to make way for the 'legal owners' of the country was 'the logical conclusion'. Or in the 1980 words of a Gush Emunim spokesman from Kiryat Arba: 'The Arabs must know that there is a master here, the Jewish people. It rules over Eretz Yisrael ... The Arabs are temporary dwellers ... There are commandments in the Bible concerning such temporary dwellers and we should act accordingly.'

The Six Day War, with its extension of Israeli control over the post-1948 residue of Palestine, gave new impetus to the notion of transfer, Israel now controlling a vast new pool of potential transferees. In November 1967, Moshe Dotan, a prominent right-winger, announced a transfer plan which he described as 'humane, healthy and just ... an act of preventative medicine'. According to Masalha, for Dotan 'every Palestinian on either side of the Green Line was a potential candidate for transfer'. The target destinations for the departees were 'the wide open spaces of Australia, Canada and Latin America' which needed settlers. The 'emigration' of some 600,000–700,000 Palestinians over a few years, Dotan argued, would dramatically change the demographic balance, achieving a Jewish majority of five to one in the Land of Greater Israel. Though possibly a 'brutal solution', it would prove 'efficient for all', a project with 'political, demographic and humanitarian implications … likely to ensure the future and the character' of Greater Israel.

Dotan's position rested on getting rid of Palestinians, basically to any country that would have them. A refinement of this theme lay in the 'Jordan is Palestine' argument. Some of those pushing this idea expressed regret that Israel had not seized the initiative straight after the 1967 war to sort out the demographic issue once and for all. One advocate wrote in a World Zionist Organization publication in the early 1980s that such a line 'would have saved us the bitter and dangerous conflict ever since which we could have already terminated by giving [sic] Jordan to the Palestinians'.

As with the drive for settlements, the appeal of transfer and the concept of 'Jordan is Palestine' was not confined to Israel's ideological right. Nur Masalha quoted Yitzhak Rabin as stating in 1973:

The problem of the Gaza refugees should not be solved in Gaza and not in El Arish [in Egypt], but in the East Bank [i.e. Jordan] … I want to create in the course of the next 10 to 20 years conditions which would cause natural migration of population to the East Bank.

In a later interview, Rabin stated 'there is a need for a place to which it would be possible to transfer a quarter of a million refugees who are residing in crowded conditions in the Gaza Strip. Such a place can only be Jordan.' Rabin, Masalha has argued, believed in 'creeping' transfer — the creation of conditions 'that would cause the residents of the occupied territories to leave'. Rabin's belief that it would be possible 'to bring about population shift on a basis other than the use of force' found echoes in Shlomo Gazit's evolving view. In 1981 he had argued that the 'problem of the Arabs of the historic Land of Israel' must be found 'outside the territories of the historic Land of Israel'. Seven years later, he described transfer as an 'entirely false messianism', although he still favoured 'voluntary' and 'agreed' transfer.

Throughout the 1980s, Masalha wrote, many commentators inside and outside Israel were frequently attempting to answer two major questions — under what circumstances should mass expulsion take place, and in what form? There were several possibilities. Transfer 'could accompany a war between Israel and an Arab country (or countries)'.[1] In a no-war situation, a policy of mass expulsion could be attempted 'in retaliation' for an escalation of Palestinian 'terrorism' and violent resistance to Israel's policies. Or, in the event of the international community being preoccupied with other crises and events, 'Israeli leaders might be tempted to carry out a partial depopulation'. Alternatively, the Israeli government 'could continue with its policy of creating ghetto conditions of daily life for Palestinians ... to force the Palestinians to migrate'.

In keeping with Israel's well-developed argumentative streak there were, and are, highly vocal opponents of transfer. Masalha noted that this was 'voiced by a large number of liberal and left-wing journalists, academics, writers and politicians, using practical and moral arguments to denounce the solution'. One academic commented that an 'Israel that would expel its Arab inhabitants would be a totalitarian-fascist state'. Critics portrayed transfer as a 'dangerous illusion', enflaming feeling towards Israel in the Arab world. One journalist wrote that it would create an 'aggressive belt of refugee camps' around Israel's borders.

Hopes for peace during the 1990s, and of the eventual creation of a viable Palestinian state in Gaza and the West Bank, marginalised the concept of transfer and its proponents. With those hopes now dashed, transfer has crept back on to the Israeli political agenda. In early 2003, three small right-wing political parties called on Palestinians to take 'a blessed journey to the Palestinian state [Jordan] which has existed for a while ... Just as our people emigrated from the Arab States to Israel, you will emigrate to the Arab states'. The parties added thoughtfully, 'We wish you successful absorption in your new home'.

Masalha has commented that the Palestinians 'have good reason to fear the threat of mass expulsions. Developments in the 1980s showed that a large section of the Likud establishment and about half of Israeli Jews openly supported the idea of "transferring" the Palestinians from the occupied territories.' Most political groups on the extreme right, 'would like to expel not just the inhabitants of the West Bank and Gaza, but also the Arab citizens of Israel'. A 2004 report by the Brussels-based International Crisis Group (ICG) noted that in a March 2002 poll, '31 per cent of Israel's Jewish population favoured transferring Palestinian citizens [of Israel] out of the country — up from 24 per cent in 1991. Some 60 per cent said they favoured encouraging them to leave.' The report quoted the uncompromising remarks from Israel's minister of transportation, Avigdor Lieberman:

> If you ask me Israel's number one problem ... is first of all Arab citizens of the State of Israel. Those who identify as Palestinians will have to move to Palestine [many would likely argue they already live there]. Do I consider them citizens of the State of Israel? No! Do we have a score to settle with them? Yes!

The idea of transfer may still be entertained mostly on the fringes of Israeli politics, but its devotees can take heart from the messages beamed to them from influential figures in the US. The Miami-based millionaire Dr Irving Moskowitz wrote in 1990 that population 'exchange' was the only real hope for a 'durable solution' of the Arab-Israeli conflict. Since the mid-1990s he has facilitated the 'transfer' of Jewish settlers to East Jerusalem by part-funding housing for them.

More important, perhaps, is the mind-set of some influential American 'neo-cons'. Writing in the *Journal of Palestine Studies* in 2004, Kathleen Christison, a former CIA policy analyst, noted that two figures in the Bush administration, Richard Perle and Douglas Feith (the latter currently Undersecretary for Policy in the Department of Defence), had contributed to a 1996 strategy paper prepared for the new Israeli prime minister, Benjamin Netanyahu. The paper advocated 'breaking away from the peace process and specifically its land-for-peace component'. Feith, Christison wrote, had 'seldom if ever deviated from a basic position that opposes territorial compromise by Israel, regards the land-for-peace concept as a step towards Israel's destruction, and believes that the only legitimate location for a Palestinian state is Jordan'. In September 2002, she noted, Perle had briefed Pentagon officials on the shape of the Middle East after a war in Iraq, displaying 'a graphic allotting all of Palestine to Israel and labeling Jordan as Palestine'.[2]

The issue of transfer goes to the heart of the identity of the Jewish state, a heart seriously congested by the blockages of occupation and demography. Israelis have long known that they cannot be at once an occupier, a democracy, and a Jewish state. As occupiers they are being outbred; if they are outbred and apply democratic principles in 'Greater' Israel they will end up as a minority in a non-Jewish nation. In mid-2003, Avraham Burg set out the hard choices this way:

> Do you want the greater Land of Israel? No problem. Abandon democracy. Let's institute an efficient system of racial separation … with prison camps and detention villages … Ghetto and Gulag …
>
> Do you want a Jewish majority? No problem. Either put the Arabs on railway cars, buses, camels and donkeys and expel them en masse — separate ourselves from them absolutely, without tricks or gimmicks. There is no middle path. We must remove all the settlements — all of them — and draw an internationally recognized border between the Jewish national home and the Palestinian national home …
>
> Do you want democracy? No problem. Either abandon the greater Land of Israel, to the last settlement and outpost, or give

full citizenship and voting rights to everyone, including Arabs. The result, of course, will be that those who did not want a Palestinian state alongside us will have one in our midst, via the ballot box.

In October 2003, Israel's choices were put equally bluntly by the historian Tony Judt. In the *New York Review of Books* he described Israel as 'not just an anachronism but a dysfunctional one', faced with three unattractive options:

- Dismantle the settlements and return to the 1967 borders within which Jews constitute a clear majority, thus remaining 'both a Jewish state and a democracy, albeit with a constitutionally anomalous community of second-class Arab citizens'.
- Continue to occupy the West Bank and Gaza, whose Arab population — added to that of present-day Israel — will become the demographic majority within five to eight years. In that case, Israel would be 'either a Jewish state (with an ever-larger majority of unenfranchised non-Jews) or it will be a democracy ... logically it cannot be both'.
- Keep the occupied territories but get rid of the Arab population, 'either by forcible expulsion or else by starving them of land and livelihood', leaving them no choice but exile. Israel would thereby remain both Jewish and at least formally democratic, but at the cost of becoming 'the first modern democracy to conduct full-scale ethnic

cleansing as a state project', something which would forever mark it as 'an outlaw state, an international pariah'.

For good measure, Judt warned that anyone who supposed
the third option as unthinkable had 'not been watching the
steady accretion of settlements and land seizures in the West
Bank over the past quarter-century'. Nor had they been listening
to the generals and politicians on the Israeli right, 'some of them
currently in government', who anticipated removal of the Arabs
'as the ineluctable condition for the survival of the Jewish state'.
The 'true alternative' in coming years would be 'between an eth-
nically cleansed Greater Israel and a single, integrated … state of
Jews and Palestinians'. What sensible Israelis fear, Judt wrote,
'much more than Hamas or the al-Aqsa Brigade is the steady
emergence of an Arab majority in "Greater Israel" and above all
the erosion of the political culture and civic morale of their
society'.

The idea of a bi-national state is anything but new. Its appeal
for the Palestinians was underscored in early 2004 when prime
minister Ahmed Qurei warned that Palestinians would 'go for a
one-state solution' if Israel unilaterally imposed new bound-
aries. The demographics speak for themselves. Even without
their own problematic 'right of return,' the Palestinian population of a single state — around 3.5 million in the West Bank and
Gaza plus another 1.2 million in present-day Israel — would
soon achieve numerical ascendancy over Israel's 5.5 million
Jews. Even without the unwelcome notion of a unitary state,
Israel is drowning demographically in its neighbourhood. In

barely over a generation, whether or not a Palestinian state exists in Gaza or the West Bank, there will be as many Palestinians in those territories as there are Israeli Jews.

In an article in May 1981 entitled *Revisiting Zionism*, Gershom Schocken of *Ha'aretz* newspaper argued that the very fact that he could sit in the garden of his house in Tel Aviv writing an item for a Hebrew daily newspaper testified 'to the soundness of the achievements of Zionism'. But, he continued, Zionism had not solved 'the Jewish problem', which continued 'to exist as before'. The major reason, he said, that Zionism had not achieved its goal was 'that the Jews, for the most part, refused to adopt the Zionist idea'. The movement had not succeeded 'in bringing more than 20 percent of the Jewish people to the state of Israel'. This basic fact

> must be the starting point for charting a new course for Zionists and citizens of the state of Israel. The differences among the various Zionist doctrines ... are no longer of any practical importance. What is important is that for one hundred years, the many-sided Zionist idea did not succeed in recruiting more than a small part of the Jewish population scattered throughout the world.

Two decades on, how should Zionism's success be judged against the criterion suggested by Schocken? In 2004, some 42 per cent of the world's Jewish population lives in Israel. It is also home to a majority of Jewish children under 15 (an important pointer to future reproductivity). These figures should give

Israelis reasonable cause for satisfaction. But they tell them also that a majority of the world's Jews remain sufficiently uninspired by Zionism as to not head for the Jewish state.

That is by no means all negative. The Diaspora remains of vital importance in shaping national attitudes and policies towards Israel — the American Jewish community is, after all, almost the size of Israel's own Jewish population. But the fast-approaching demographic D-day raises two vital questions: will it inspire Diaspora Jews to pack their bags and head for the Jewish state; and how will those Jews already living in Israel respond?

Israel's current economic woes and the bloody conflict with the Palestinians are blamed for a dramatic slump in new arrivals over the past few years. There were only 23,000 in 2003, the lowest figure since 1988. This bad news is compounded by the departure from Israel of Jewish arrivals from the former Soviet Union. Around 7 per cent of the nearly one million who arrived have since relocated, mainly to Canada, the US or Europe. The worst-case demographic scenario for Israel combines a drying-up of immigration and a steady haemorrhage of its disillusioned citizens. The clock is ticking.

But the population time-bomb and the troublesome neighbourhood are only part of contemporary Israel's dilemma. To them must be joined the one phenomenon that, more than any other, accounted for the creation of the Jewish state in the first place — that of anti-Semitism. Here, there is a profound and multi-layered paradox. Herzl, and those with him, saw the Jewish homeland as the only effective counter to anti-Semitism, the one way of putting Jews beyond the reach of those who would do them harm solely because of their Jewishness. However, even after the obscene violence of the Holocaust, only a minority of the world's Jews actually sought the sanctuary of the Jewish state. The reasons for this were various, but in part lay in the reality that many Jews probably felt safer at some distance from Israel. And, despite Schocken's regret at Zionism's failure to recruit more immigrants, there were substantial pluses for the Jewish state in having active supporters scattered around the globe.

Today another element of the paradox is on display. It centres on the question of whether the actions of the Jewish state fuel anti-Semitism; whether criticism of Israeli policies is little more than a mask for anti-Semitic utterings. A 2003 poll conducted in European Union states reported that 59 per cent of Europeans saw Israel as a threat to world peace — ahead of Iran, North Korea and the US, who all registered 53 per cent on the 'Eurobarometer', followed by Iraq, Afghanistan and Pakistan. (Eight per cent of respondents described the EU itself as a threat.) The poll was seized on by Jewish groups and Israeli government representatives as proof positive of the rising tide of anti-Semitism within Europe. The Israeli Embassy in Brussels declared that Europeans had 'put the Jewish state below the level of the worst pariah state and terror organizations'. It was 'not only sad but outraged. Not at European citizens,' the embassy added diplomatically, rather 'at those who are responsible for forming public opinion'.

Is opposition to Israeli policy, or concern about its longer-term impact, the same as anti-Semitism? Natan Sharansky, the former Soviet dissident and Israeli government minister, certainly seems to think so. In November 2003, he wrote in *Commentary* that an increasing number of people, 'including some Jews, are convinced that anti-Semitism will end only with the *disappearance* of the Jewish state'. The notion that the world 'increasingly hates Jews because it hates Israel', that Israel 'is one of the primary causes of anti-Semitism, if not *the* primary cause,' he said, had 'gained much currency'. Israel, he went on, obviously could not 'be the cause of a phenomenon that predates it by over 2,000 years'.

That is a reasonable deduction. But Sharansky unabashedly conflates criticism of Israel with anti-Semitism. When Israel conformed, he wrote, 'to the template of the world's moralizers' during the 1990s it was rewarded: 'Sure enough, worldwide indices of anti-Semitism … dropped to their lowest point since the Holocaust'. Now, criticism is rising, as are the indices of anti-Semitism. So criticism must equal anti-Semitism — end of argument. Or is it? What Sharansky seems to imply is that anti-Semites had cause for hope for Israel's demise in the 1990s, since, in his words, it had extended

its hand to a terrorist organization still committed to its destruction, … agreed to the establishment of a dictatorial and repressive regime on its very doorstep, sustaining its commitment to the so-called peace process no matter how many innocent Jews were killed and wounded in its fraudulent name.

But the nexus between criticism and anti-Semitism is a good deal more complex than Sharansky wants to believe. Take his comments and compare them to these:

> if we do not turn away from this path of adhering to the entire Land of Israel, and if we do not also begin to understand the other side ... we will get nowhere. We must, once and for all, admit there is another side ... that it is suffering, and that we are behaving disgracefully ... there is no other word for it. Disgracefully.

These words come not from some virulent overseas critic or rabid anti-Semite. They come from none other than Avraham Shalom, one of *four* former heads of Israel's internal security service who have been highly, and publicly, critical of Israel's handling of the Palestinian question. Presumably, in a future issue of *Commentary*, Sharansky will lambast Shalom and his colleagues' anti-Semitic sentiments.

During a 2003 discussion in New York on anti-Semitism, the Dutch historian Ian Buruma, who is of Jewish origin, warned of the dangers of too often crying 'gevalt' about anti-Semitism. This Yiddish exclamation is probably best translated here as 'Oh no', or 'Not again!' Earlier, Buruma had captured some of the complexities involved in the debate over anti-Semitism when he wrote in *The Guardian*:

> Not every Jew is a Zionist, nor is every Zionist a Jew ... it is perfectly possible to be an anti-Semitic Zionist ... While there are

plainly anti-Zionists who are also anti-Semites, you can be anti-Zionist without being anti-Semitic. Plenty of Jews don't like the idea of a Jewish state; some even actively oppose it.

Uri Avinery is a former Israeli parliamentarian and veteran peace activist. In January 2004 he posed this question: 'Is everybody who criticises Israel an anti-Semite?' His reply? 'Absolutely not. Absolutely not.' Avinery drew the vital distinction between those who criticised Israel 'for certain of our actions' and those who hate Israel 'because it is the Jewish state'. The former 'cannot be accused of anti-Semitism'. The latter were anti-Semitic. Avinery noted that it was not always easy to distinguish between the two, because 'shrewd anti-Semites pose as bona fide critics of Israel's actions'. But in Europe, he said, the number of anti-Semites had not grown; 'perhaps it has even fallen'. What had increased was 'the volume of criticism of Israel's behaviour towards the Palestinians, who appear as "the victims of the victims" '. Presenting all critics of Israel as anti-Semites, he wrote, was wrong and counterproductive, and damaged 'the fight against anti-Semitism. Many deeply moral persons criticise our behaviour in the occupied territories. It is stupid to accuse them of anti-Semitism.'

Jabotinsky once observed that, as a colonising adventure, Zionism would stand or fall on the question of armed force. He noted pithily that, important as it was to build and to speak Hebrew, it was 'even more important to be able to shoot'. Ultimately, however, Israel has to rest on more than shot and shell, on chutzpah and argument — and on more than scattergun accusations of 'anti-Semitism' to blunt its critics. The danger of labelling every critic an enemy is that they might become just that.

CHAPTER SIX

Palestinian fantasies

For two decades after 1967 the Palestinians attacked a country they liked to pretend did not exist. Finally it dawned on them that it did, and was most likely there to stay. So, in November 1988, Arafat, then based in Tunis, proclaimed 'the creation of the State of Palestine with Holy Jerusalem as its capital'. Unlikely as it may seem, that amounted to formal recognition of the Jewish state. For Arafat's declaration also included acceptance of UN Security Council Resolutions 242 and 338. The first had been drawn up after the Six Day War in 1967; the second, after the 1973 Arab-Israeli conflict. They called for Israeli withdrawal from territories occupied during these conflicts and for Arab states to respect Israel's right to live in peace in the region.[1]

By signing on to these two resolutions, Arafat, at least implicitly, accepted Israel's place in the region. Five years later, Arafat and Israeli prime minister Rabin exchanged letters. Arafat's confirmed 'the right of the State of Israel to exist in peace and security' and that 'those articles of the Palestinian Covenant which deny Israel's right to exist … are now inoperative and no longer valid'. Rabin's brief letter advised that

Israel 'has decided to recognize the PLO as the representative of the Palestinian people and commence negotiations'. And so the 'Oslo' peace process was born.

It would come to nought: Rabin was murdered in 1995; new violence erupted in 2000, with Arafat finally holed up in the West Bank city of Ramallah; and thick seams of new hatred and suspicion and a thirst for vengeance were laid down. Could it have been different had Rabin lived? Could it have been different had Arafat risen above his determined instinct to be all things to all people? Could the difference between peace and today's reality be distilled into a lack of body armour for Rabin and a shave and good suit for Arafat?

Even during the 1990s, we should remind ourselves, the peacemakers held one hand behind their back: Rabin giving the thumbs up to the settlement builders; Arafat holding a blindfold, which he conveniently slipped on to avoid seeing those planning terrorist outrages against Israel. They could not deal with each other as equals because they were not. Palestinians saw themselves as negotiating the terms of their final surrender. What they saw as 'justice' long denied — that is, the return of Palestinian land and the prospect of an eventual, though highly truncated state — Israelis saw as major 'concession'. Given where the two sides were coming from, both were right.

In a caustic response to Tony Judt's article, the head of the American 'Anti-Defamation League', Abraham Foxman, applauded Israel's moderate positions, including its 'overwhelming readiness to make significant concessions on territory and settlements despite the murderous intentions of its neighbours'. But, Palestinians would argue, 'how can the return of our land and the removal from it of a few Jewish settlers be trumpeted by any reasonable person as a concession — should a thief be acclaimed for returning stolen goods?'

Neither during the 1990s, nor before, and certainly not since, did either side make any sustained effort to change the underlying mentality of the conflict. A few examples give an insight. After Israel's formal annexation of East Jerusalem in 1967, it recognised pre-1948 Jewish property rights not just in East Jerusalem, but elsewhere in the West Bank. There was no similar recognition of Palestinian property rights in Israel — to the victor the spoils. Despite Arafat's 1988 proclamation and the 1993 exchange of letters, as late as September 2000 the Palestinian Authority could not bring itself to mention Israel by name in new school textbooks. Only a few months earlier, to his credit, the Israeli education minister, Yossi Sarid, had tried to include the Palestinian nationalist poet Mahmoud Darwish in the Israeli school curriculum. For this assault on Israeli sensibilities, Ehud Barak's ailing Labour-led government was threatened with a no-confidence motion.

When Israeli settlers describe Arabs as 'donkeys', and Palestinians acclaim as heroic 'martyrs' those who brutally murder Israelis, they are simply reflecting the view of the other that has built up over generations. Few on either side have had the courage, or the tenacity, to try to change this. The terrible events of the past four years have not merely hardened these mind-sets; they have calcified them.

The Palestinians have been accused of many sins of omission

and commission. Some of the more outlandish ones include being held partly responsible for the Holocaust. In *The Case for Israel* the US lawyer Alan Dershowitz asserted that some 'Arab and Palestinian leaders bore significant responsibility for the Holocaust. They supported it, aided it, used it to their advantage, and expected to benefit from it.' This was too much for an otherwise flattering reviewer in the *Jerusalem Post*, Daniel Gordis. Although he held the book to be a 'profound contribution to an extraordinary country now in dire straits', Dershowitz's passion had got 'the better of him'. Gordis added wryly that while there was 'much of which the Arabs can be accused; adding the Shoah [Holocaust] to the list seems a bit of a stretch'. Dershowitz might usefully have noted Hannah Arendt's comment in her book *Eichmann in Jerusalem*, that the trial revealed that 'all' the rumours about Eichmann's 'connection with Haj Amin el Husseini, the former Mufti of Jerusalem, were unfounded'.

Dershowitz overstated his case. This is nothing new when it comes to Palestine. There the 'game' is played for keeps — politically, territorially, and morally. There, no quarter is given, and rarely is any effort made to comprehend the concerns, the hopes, or the fears of the other side. Amos Elon, a staunch critic of much Israeli policy, has rightly expressed despair at the absence of

> anyone in the Palestinian camp who was seriously concerned by the fact that the PLO was, as far as I know, the only national liberation movement in history willing to extend its ruthlessness

anywhere in the world[2] ... Nor, more recently have we heard Arafat or any Palestinian human rights group criticise the brain-washing of impressionable teenagers by 'holy men' who convince them that they would be revered as martyrs ... if only they blew themselves up in a discotheque full of other young people or in a crowded fast-food restaurant.

Elon is among a handful of those who have made a real effort to understand the mentality of the conflict. Others include Avraham Burg, Avraham Shalom, and the former attorney-general, Michael Ben-Yair, who has described the current intifada as 'the Palestinian people's war of national liberation. Historical processes', he added, 'teach us that no nation is prepared to live under another's domination and that a suppressed people's war of national liberation will inevitably succeed. We understand this point but choose to ignore it.' To this brief list we might also add Shlomo Ben-Ami, Israel's foreign minister in Ehud Barak's short-lived government, who once observed: 'Maybe what we lacked was not time. Maybe we lacked the readiness of both parties to reconcile themselves to the most vital myths of the other.'

Too often, however, such voices of moderation are drowned by rampant, self-righteous indignation. Constantly, it seems the excesses of one side — both of word and deed — cross-fertilise those of the other. Moreover, what few voices of reason there are seem mostly to exist on the Israeli side. While they are not absent among Palestinians, too often they are quiescent. This is not simply a matter of the Israelis being technologically better equipped or more accomplished at communicating their message. The absence of a moderate Palestinian voice demonstrates not only the controlling nature of Arafat's rule, but the overriding mentality among Palestinians of being both the victim and the vanquished, of being beyond compromise.

Yet no issue demands further compromise more than the 'right of return' for Palestinian refugees. It is not, as some Israelis and their supporters suggest, because the problem was entirely of the Palestinians' own making. Efraim Karsh, from the University of London, has argued, for example, that if the Palestinians and the Arab world had accepted the UN partition plan 'and not sought to subvert it by force of arms there would have been no refugee problem in the first place'. As a statement of perfect hindsight that is probably true. But it also conveniently airbrushes the deliberate expulsion of Palestinians by Israel's founders, and rests on the quite extraordinary assumption that Palestinians should have embraced their 'relocation' as a selfless contribution towards the creation of the Jewish state. That said, if we take Arafat's 1988 acknowledgement of Israel's right to exist, plus his exchange of letters with Rabin in 1993, and place them alongside the continuing insistence on a fully fledged right of return for Palestinian refugees, Israeli suspicions about ultimate Palestinian intentions are readily understandable.

As with Israel's other demographic anxieties, the numbers speak for themselves. In the course of the 1948 Arab-Israeli war some 700,000 Palestinians, or about two-thirds of the total Palestinian population, were uprooted. The total, with descendants, now hovers around four million people (some claims put it substantially higher), living in Jordan, Gaza, the West Bank, Syria, and Lebanon. One does not need to be a mathematician to understand the implications of a fully fledged Palestinian 'right of return'. Depending on the precise numbers, either overnight, or nearly overnight, it would destroy Israel as a Jewish state.

Not surprisingly, then, this issue unites Israelis across the political spectrum, including ardent advocates of a two-state solution. Yossi Sarid might have wanted to put Mahmoud Darwish on the school curriculum, but he commented in 2001 that Israel could not survive 'the right of return'. The leading author Amos Oz — castigated as a bleeding heart by some fellow Israelis — has described the right of return as a means of 'eradicating Israel'. Avraham Burg observed that his family's deep links with Hebron were 'cruelly severed' by the 1929 massacre there. This had forever divided his family: 'One half will never again trust a Palestinian. The other half will never stop searching for neighbours who seek peace.' Burg added:

> I compromise with my dream of returning to Hebron in order that I may live free in the new Israel. And my Palestinian brother must give up his dream of returning to Jaffa in order to live an honourable and dignified life in Nablus. Only those capable of compromising with their dreams can sit together to forge a compromise on behalf of their nations.

A few Palestinians understand the need for compromise. In 2001, the Israeli peace activist, Gershon Baskin, wrote that:

in all my intensive talks with Palestinian leaders … I found a lot of understanding that the right of return of Palestinian refugees was not a real option … all spoke of the need for Israel to recognise the principle of the right of return and then to negotiate the implementation in such a way that would lead the refugees to settle in the Palestinian state or stay where they are.

Some Palestinians and Israelis have shown a preparedness to reach across the divide. In 2002, the leading Palestinian intellectual Sari Nusseibeh, and a former head of Israel's internal security service, Ami Ayalon, jointly developed a 'People's Voice' peace plan resting on the principles of 'two states for two peoples'. It called for permanent borders based on the 4 June 1967 lines (that is, before the outbreak of the Six Day War); 'no' settlers remaining in the Palestinian state; and the 'open city' of Jerusalem as the capital of the two states. On the right of return, it declared that Palestinian refugees would return only to the state of Palestine; Jews would return only to the State of Israel. In recognition of the 'suffering and the plight' of Palestinian refugees, the international community, Israel, and the Palestinian state would contribute to an international fund to compensate them.

Ayalon warned that, if Israel were to be a safe home for the Jewish people, 'there must be a Palestinian state … the Palestinians must have hope and feel secure'. For his part, Nusseibeh told fellow Palestinians that it was 'not enough to cry and write poetry'. Some 180,000 Israelis and 140,000 Palestinians signed petitions in support of the plan.

In 2003, the 'Geneva Accord' was developed by the former Israeli justice minister Yossi Beilin and the former Palestinian minister for information and culture Yasser Abed-Rabbo. It repeated the call for Palestinians to relinquish the right of return, proposed the evacuation of around half the West Bank settlers, and outlined a sharing of control in East Jerusalem under international supervision.

It is near impossible to imagine a future settlement of the Israeli-Palestinian conflict that does not rest heavily on the principles suggested in these separate but overlapping proposals. But the fundamental issue remains that of translating worthy ideals into positive facts-on-the-ground, of changing the mentality of the conflict, of reshaping how most Israelis and Palestinians, not just a sophisticated few, view each other — of teaching people how to forget. 'The Palestinian-Israeli conflict is characterized by deep fault lines and deeply entrenched positions', commented Ami Isseroff, an Israeli peace activist, on the Geneva Accord. Israelis would 'not necessarily give up Jerusalem or Ariel [a major West Bank settlement] just because Yossi Beilin signed a paper saying they would'.

Ironically, President Bush's declaration in early 2004 that 'a just, fair, and realistic' solution lay in settling Palestinian refugees in 'a Palestinian state ... rather than in Israel' may have hardened official Palestinian thinking on this issue. The Palestinian Prime Minister, Ahmed Qurei, warned in response that no one could 'renounce ... the right of return'. Khaled al-Batsh, a senior Islamic Jihad official, put it more forthrightly. Ignoring the Palestinian refugees' right of return, he said, amounted to 'a declaration of war against our people'. This may only be posturing. But the end result is the same — a deepening of suspicion about whether the Palestinians really are interested in a two-state solution.

Alon Ben-Meir, professor of international relations at New York University, wrote in April 2004 that the Palestinian Authority had 'been engaged in serious public deception by claiming it seeks only 23 percent of the former British Mandate of Palestine — made up of the West Bank and Gaza — but in the same breath demanding the right of return'. He argued that the authority needed to understand that, 'regardless of the validity of the Palestinian right of return, when survival itself is the issue, the question of what is right or wrong is barely relevant'. The demographic reality was simple

with only 5.5 million Jews living in Israel, if it is to absorb nearly 4 million Palestinian refugees in addition to the 1.5 million Palestinians who are already Israeli citizens, the Palestinians will become a majority almost immediately, even without any influx of Palestinians from the West Bank and Gaza ... [Such a reality would] obliterate Israel as a Jewish state.

Palestinian leaders can point to UN General Assembly Resolution 194, passed in December 1948 and ritually re-affirmed ever since. This declared that refugees 'wishing to return to their homes and live at peace with their neighbours should be permitted to do so at the earliest practical date,' with compensation being 'paid for the property of those choosing not to return and for the loss or damage of property'. Almost 60 years on, this is a statement of the aggrieved; its practical import is nil. As long as Palestinian leaders persist with the 'misguided dream' of a fully fledged return, to use Alon Ben-Meir's words, they hold out to the refugees a fantasy solution.

In his 1991 study of Palestinian dispossession, *The People of Nowhere*, Israeli journalist Danny Rubinstein commented that, as long as refugees 'insisted upon actually returning to their homes and lands … there was no chance' of a negotiated settlement with Israel. A detailed report issued in 2004 by the International Crisis Group commented that, even after the PLO's 'strategic shift toward … a negotiated two-state settlement … it never repudiated its official commitment to the right of return'.[3] Some Palestinian officials had

informally proposed solutions … consistent with separate Palestinian Arab and Israeli Jewish states — thereby acknowledging a fundamental incompatibility between a negotiated two-state solution and unrestricted implementation of refugee demands.

The Palestinian leadership 'reacted ambivalently, alternately ignoring the issue and confirming its pro forma commitment to the right of return'. The ICG's advice to the leadership was diplomatically couched, but the clear message was that it needed to move on. An internal Palestinian dialogue was 'crucial and long overdue'; a resolution would need to be based 'on repatriation to a Palestinian state, normalisation of status in host countries, relocation to third-countries, symbolic return to Israel and compensation'.

But can the Palestinian leadership move on, not only on the critical matter of refugees, but also on the mentality of the conflict? Will it dare cut a deal with the state that has brought so much uncertainty and misery into Palestinian life for the past five-and-a-half decades? Have the Palestinians become, if not comfortable, at least so used to the notion of 'victimhood' that they will not risk changing it? In his controversial article, *Israel: The Alternative*, Judt argued that the problem for the Jewish state was not that it was 'a European "enclave" in the Arab world' but rather that it 'arrived too late'. At least it arrived.

A bigger problem for the Palestinians, their region and the wider world may be that their state does not arrive at all, or arrives in such a way as to make a mockery of the notion of statehood. This is not simply because the notion of joining Gaza and a few bits of the West Bank will pose a geographic nightmare, but also because Palestinians may be so obsessed with the trauma of their 'liberation struggle' that vengeance — encouraged by the memory of the quixotic Arafat — will remain the highest individual and national goal.

And even assuming there might, one day, be a Palestinian state, encompassing Gaza and most of the West Bank, who will rule it? Will they be the successors to Arafat's Fatah and the PLO, with their broadly secular outlook on the world? Or will the struggle for statehood have swept them aside, installing those who 'rightly' represent the Muslim people of Palestine? The religious radicalisation of the conflict, the fading of its essentially nationalist dynamic, is making it even more insoluble.

For 30-plus years — through manipulation, expulsion, bribery and assassination — Israel has tried to create a quiescent Palestinian leadership which will largely do its bidding. Now it is waiting for a 'reliable Palestinian partner'. A January 2004 ICG report commented succinctly that this is 'a recipe for paralysis, or worse: only a credible political process can produce an effective Palestinian leadership, not the other way around'.

The irony is that it suits both Palestinian and Israeli to have hardliners in charge on the other side. This provides just the rationale for inaction, and worse. Martin Indyk reportedly once commented that Arafat was 'Israel's best hope ... since the alternative was Hamas or Hezbollah'. But unless we can imagine Likud and Hamas in bed together, we cannot imagine a solution to the Israeli-Palestinian conflict.

And what of the sheer practicalities, the need to run a Palestinian civic society, the need to put out the garbage and build the roads and create the jobs and feed the people? What of the vital, though ruptured, economic linkages between 'Palestine' and Israel, and the pressing need for them to agree on how water as well as land should be shared? Can Palestinians be 'retrained' for peace? We hear so much of 'capacity building'; who will perform this task in Palestine? Will it be Israel — which has the greatest physical incentive and the sharpest psychological disincentive? Will it be the dislocated Arab world, which champions the Palestinian cause when it suits, but which will increasingly be troubled by the pain of its own sclerotic authoritarianism? Will it be the Europeans, with their long record in the Middle East of high-minded duplicity? Or will it be the Americans, with their particular agendas to pursue and axes to grind?

Commenting on Israel's mooted withdrawal from Gaza, Indyk observed that, ideally, 'a responsible Palestinian government would emerge in Gaza with an effective security force that would take control of the settlements, disarm the terrorist organizations and armed gangs, and police the borders and entry points'. Then he added that 'the moon is closer to the earth' than the Palestinians in Gaza were to achieving this. Even if the Palestinians have a state, will it be a failed one before it begins? Is it too late for normalcy, for the mundane, everyday tasks that states and their leaders have to perform? Is it too late for Palestine?

CHAPTER SEVEN

Apocalypse soon?

R onald Storrs, the then British military governor of Jerusalem, once declared: 'Two hours of Arab grievances drive me to the synagogue ... after an intensive course of Zionist propaganda I am prepared to embrace Islam'. For more than a century, the contest between Jew and Palestinian has driven many others to similar distraction. Can there be two peoples anywhere more absorbed with their own rightness — their own 'question' — so consumed by their own myths, so dismissive of the other, so constant in demonising their neighbour and delegitimising their cause, so stubborn in their denial of a common destiny?

Israelis and Palestinians are both victims — of history and of each other's physical aggression and absolutist mentality. They are locked tight in a world where they see only the slivers of glass under their own skin, never the wounds of another people who have been wronged and cheated and hurt, and who must somehow be accommodated, even at the risk of limiting their own dreams. The two communities live alongside each other, wrote Danny Rubinstein in 1991; they 'inhabit the same country, yet the cultural and psychological distance between them is immense'.

Once, as a diplomat, I was encouraged to believe we should always look for solutions, no matter how dark and complex the situation. For a time, in the early 1990s, this approach seemed vindicated. In a process of extraordinary change, South Africa threw off the shackles of apartheid, freeing both bodies and minds. Yitzhak Rabin and Yasser Arafat shook hands on the White House lawn. That time now seems like a dream, almost as distant as the utopian world portrayed in Herzl's novel *Altneuland*. Now, on what Tony Judt has described as 'the corpse-strewn landscape of the Fertile Crescent,' Ariel Sharon, Yasser Arafat, and a handful of terrorists 'can all claim victory, and they do'. But worse is the fact that the bloodstained streets of Israel and of Palestine will not miraculously be cleansed with the departure of Sharon and Arafat. For, as much as a cause, they are a symptom — of the myopia, the intolerance, and the inhumanity which has held the peoples of Palestine in a vice-like grip for the past one hundred years. And which beset them still.

Zionism was driven by the perceived need for Jews to disengage from Europe. In pursuing this aim they engaged with another people. At first, many Zionists tried hard not to see them. Ultimately, in 1967, they would conquer them. In 2004, Israel wants to disengage from all of these people but only part of the land. That painful and bloody contradiction runs deep. Yaron Ezrahi wrote in *Rubber Bullets*:

> Since 1967 ... the romantic idea of the Israeli army — of armed Jews fighting to secure historic, religious, or metaphysical justice for the Jewish people — has become demystified by individual

Jews' experiences of killing and being killed in wars, as well as the moral ambiguities and ideological contradictions inherent in the encounter between a vision of liberation and the realities of conquest.

If the romance has died, can the state muster the fortitude and the sense of purpose to go on protecting itself indefinitely? The *Ha'aretz* journalist Gideon Levy has urged soldiers serving in the territories to speak out, 'to tell the truth … to relate how they killed and jailed and humiliated for no good reason'. Israel, Levy wrote, was still a very long time from establishing a truth and reconciliation commission. It would come, but 'in the meantime story hour has already arrived'.

If, by some miracle, Herzl came back today, what would he think? His naïve hope was that all Jews would settle in the Jewish state, and that this would end anti-Semitism through the abolition of the Diaspora. If he had known that this would never be the case, that one hundred years after his death there would be almost as many Jews in America as in Israel, would he have abandoned the quest? The Jewish state is far removed from the one he dreamed of — in which theocracy would take a back seat, the flag would proclaim merely the virtues of hard work, and a babble of languages would flow. Would Herzl find the world's Jews safer from persecution than in his time, safer since the infamy of the Holocaust plundered their numbers?

The negatives of Israel's existence — the land and blood feud with the Palestinians, the fate of individual Jewish Israelis — can be charted. But we can only measure what has happened during Israel's existence, not what might have happened if it had not. The Jewish state is a regional, nuclear-armed superpower enjoying the occasionally qualified but never threatened support of the world's one remaining global superpower. But it is a state that has been unable to resolve the contradiction of its creation: that self-determination for one people trampled on self-determination for another.

Should we, who are non-Jewish, be content with celebrating the extraordinary intellectual, technological, and cultural stimulus that Israel has brought into our lives? Or should we more despair the fact — brought into our lives almost daily, often horrifically — that, five-and-a-half decades after the creation of the Jewish state, its citizens cannot coexist peacefully with their neighbours? And perhaps never will. It is not just about occupation and terror: it is about the studied blindness of two people to see the other, to accept that they have a legitimate place on the landscape; it is about their seeming inability to act towards the other in a way that might reduce, not enlarge, the pool of hatred and bitterness.

If it is too late for Palestine, is it becoming too late for Israel? Given the crucial role played by the Holocaust in creating the conditions for Israel's emergence after World War II, will support for it pass with the survivors of the Holocaust? Reviewing *Death and the Nation*, a study by the Israeli historian and columnist Idith Zertal of the way the Holocaust shaped the Israeli world-view, Yitzhak Laor wrote in *Ha'aretz* that the core of the issue was the state's 'appropriation of the Holocaust ... and its transformation into a powerful instrument, not only for building the nation but for negating the national aspirations of the Palestinians, comparing them to the Nazis'. Is the memory of the Holocaust an instrument of infinite power? This, and the related issue of 'whither Israel?', are not merely academic questions. They matter not just to the Jews of Israel and the Jews of the Diaspora but to all of us. For if Israel, as the Jewish nation, loses its way, what will become of its Jews? And what will become of the Land of Israel? If, in fifty or one hundred years' time, there is no Jewish homeland, what will have taken its place?

And if we are nearing the end of the Zionist era, does that mean, by definition, we are nearing the end of Israel? A 2004 survey conducted by the Israeli Democracy Institute found that nearly half of Israeli teenagers did not feel 'part of the country and its problems'. Some 27 per cent did not think they would remain in Israel. Avraham Burg has argued that

the end of the Zionist enterprise is already on our doorstep … There may yet be a Jewish state here, but it will be a different sort, strange and ugly … We live in a thunderously failed reality. Yes, we have revived the Hebrew language, created a marvelous theater and a strong national currency. Our Jewish minds are as sharp as ever. We are traded on the Nasdaq. But is this why we created a state? … It turns out that the 2,000-year struggle for Jewish survival comes down to a state of settlements, run by an amoral clique of corrupt lawbreakers who are deaf both to their citizens and their enemies. A state lacking justice cannot survive. More and more Israelis are coming to understand this as they ask their children where they expect to live in 25 years. Children who are honest admit, to their parents' shock, that they do not know. The countdown to the end of Israeli society has begun.

In the words of Amos Elon, 'the centre has collapsed' in Israel and Palestine. The much-talked-about two-state solution may not be possible 'since on both sides all confidence is gone'. The extremists of Greater Israel and Greater Palestine 'veto all progress'.

Benny Morris is even gloomier, declaring that

> there will not be a solution. We are doomed to live by the sword ... For my children that is especially bleak. I don't know whether they will want to go on living in a place where there is not hope. Even if Israel is not destroyed, we won't see a good, normal life here in the decades ahead. ... I don't see the bombings as isolated acts ... They [the Palestinians] want what happened to the bus to happen to all of us ... Something like a cage has to be built for them ... there is no choice. There is a wild animal there that has to be locked up in one way or another ... Even though we are oppressing the Palestinians, we are the weaker side here ... Everyone will understand we are the true victims. But by then it will be too late.

To this internal debate we must add an external one, every bit as sharp and unrelenting. In July 1998, Israel's golden jubilee year, Mark Corby in *The Spectator* drew a direct parallel between the fate of the Crusaders and the one he envisaged for Israel. In retrospect, he wrote, both Crusaders and Israelis were to find that conquest 'was to prove relatively cheap and simple in comparison to the costs and complexities of occupation'. Israel's lifeline, he argued, came almost 'without qualification' from the United States, which eventually would 'tire of this burden'. In *How Israel Lost* Richard Ben Cramer wrote that he had been wrong about the prospect for peace

> because I expected Israel to act in her national interest. What I didn't see, or failed to think about, was the break-up of Israel's national consensus — the atomization of the Jewish society. What Israel lost ... was precisely the capacity to act in the national interest.

The only winner, Cramer, wrote, was 'the conflict itself'.

Earlier, two other prominent members of the American Jewish community, Norman Podhoretz and Ron Unz, had exchanged blows in the pages of *Commentary* (of which the former is editor-at-large; Unz is a Silicon valley multi-millionaire). In an October 2001 article decrying the lingering influence of the Oslo 'peacemongers', and in which he described Shimon Peres as a worse appeaser than Neville Chamberlain, Podhoretz declared that nothing that Israel could do, 'short of committing suicide — or better still weakening itself to the point where it can be wiped out in a mighty holy war ... in which all the Arab armies will participate — can satisfy the Palestinians'. Arafat was neither the problem nor the solution. Even if he died tomorrow, 'nothing would change'.

Podhoretz went on to ask whether there was any glimmer of light at the end of 'this dark and gloomy tunnel?' For the 'foreseeable future', he answered, Israel's only realistic choice was 'to hold tight, to keep its powder dry, to refine the anti-terrorist techniques it has already developed, to ensure the credibility of its military power ... and to use that power if and when the Arabs force it to'. There was a future, a time when the Arab world might 'make its *own* peace with the existence of the Jewish state ... on that day, making peace with Israel will be as easy as it is now impossible'. Recalling that 'it took more than three centuries before war between France and Germany became unthinkable,' by Podhoretz's reckoning Israel's conflict with the Arab world was 'still, relatively speaking, in an early stage'.

Unz voiced disquiet at what he saw as Podhoretz's rampant optimism. As someone 'whose grandparents helped found ... Israel', he felt 'immense sadness' after reading Podhoretz's article and demanded a reality check. The 'hardest reality' was that 'absolutely none of the proposed solutions' put forward by Israel's political parties had 'any likelihood of future success, whether the "war" proposals found on the near or far Right or the "peace" proposals found on the near or far Left'. Harking back to the original motivation for Israel's creation — Jewish insecurity in the Diaspora — Unz argued that a half-century or more 'of very good circumstances for Jews in America and other Western nations' had largely 'dissipated the pressures for Israel's existence'. And harking back even further, Unz drew the same parallel as Corby had done in *The Spectator* between the fate of Israel and the Crusaders. In a nutshell, Unz expected 'Israel's trajectory to follow that of the temporary Crusader kingdoms, surviving for seventy to eighty years following its 1948 establishment, then collapsing under continual Muslim pressure and flagging ideological commitment'.

Two points might be made about Unz's gloomy prognostication. No one can know whether it will prove correct, whether the next generation of Israelis will be the last. But even without the answer, is the fact of the debate — within the world's Jewish community just as much as outside it — an incentive to the Palestinians also to dig in, to await Israel's gradual, inexorable decline? Is it further inducement to remain immobile on the Palestinian right of return?

Podhoretz may well be right about France and Germany. But there was no demographic time-bomb ticking away between them the way it is now for Israel. Ben-Gurion thought time was on Israel's side. In hindsight, nothing could have been further from the truth. Ami Ayalon told *Le Monde* in late 2001 that, politically, time favoured 'Hamas and the settlers' and demographically worked in favour of the Palestinians. The 'womb of the Arab woman', as Arafat has indelicately put it, is one of the Palestinians' most potent weapons.

Early in 2002, in an article entitled 'Hail Caesar', the noted Israeli author David Grossman urged 'Caesar' to carry on: 'You will soon force our enemies to love us, no matter what we do to them … Only please, could you hurry up a little … we beg of you, get a move on because soon, how should we put it, you won't have any people left. Soldiers or civilians.' Later that year, Shimon Peres, who has laboured hard and long for the Israeli state, and not a little for his own glory, wrote of a deepening chasm between Israelis and Palestinians. He commented typically, 'We are sorry but not desperate'.

He might perhaps have added wisely, 'Not yet'.

CHAPTER EIGHT

Postscript: A world without Arafat—when will the dreaming end?

Arafat's legacy...the leader, the president who united the Palestinian people...who kept the Palestinian national identity from extinction.
— Palestinian cabinet minister Saeb Erekat

[It is] good that the world is rid of him...the sun is shining in the Middle East.
— [Then] Israeli cabinet minister Tommy Lapid

I regret that in 2000 he missed the opportunity to bring that [Palestinian] nation into being.
— Former US president Bill Clinton

He led his people to an historic acceptance of the need for a two-state solution.
— British prime minister Tony Blair

Every year, on 11 November, millions of people around the globe pause to remember those who endured the horrors of the First World War. A fittingly ironic date, perhaps, for Yasser Arafat to die in a Paris hospital in 2004. For he, more than anyone, had ensured that the Palestinians too would not be forgotten. Reviled by many, worshipped by some, Arafat simply could not be ignored. If a Palestinian state ever comes into being, many of its symbols will bear his name.

Arafat took his last breath some three years after Osama bin Laden's devastating attacks against America's own symbols of power. Subsequently, bin Laden cited his indignation over the plight of the Palestinians as a partial explanation for his actions. This convenient post-facto rationalisation drew a rightly sceptical response. Nabil Shaath, for example, the urbane Palestinian minister for 'planning' (read, foreign affairs), noted pithily that bin Laden had 'just remembered Palestine'.

This newfound focus on the Palestinian cause was not confined to the world's most notorious terrorist. In the wake of 9/11, president George Bush recalled that a Palestinian state had always been part of his 'vision'. In Britain, prime minister Blair declared there was an urgent need to 'seize the moment' and re-invigorate the ailing peace process. But nothing of consequence changed, and Arafat spent the last years of his life holed up in his headquarters in Ramallah. There he continued to be all things to all people: valiant liberation leader; committed peacemaker; corrupt, bloodstained deceiver. And when his time came, comment about Arafat dead, inevitably, was as wide-ranging and contradictory as about Arafat alive.

With his passing those who had cast him as the major impediment to peace began talking up the possibilities of change. President Bush commented that it was a 'significant moment' in Palestinian history. Jordan's King Abdullah, wary no doubt of the 'Jordan is Palestine' line proffered by some Israelis, expressed hope that the Palestinians would overcome the 'deep pain' of their leader's loss to establish 'an independent Palestinian state'. Ariel Sharon noted that 'recent events', as he termed them, 'could be a historic turning point for the Middle East'.

But Arafat's legacy is one of questions, not answers.

Now that the individual who most cogently embodied their distrust lies buried in Ramallah, will Israelis look upon the Palestinians with greater empathy? In their new, uncertain world, will Palestinians return this in kind? Will a conflict that has consumed lives and treasure for generations now peter out because one person has left the scene? Are we truly in a new era of peacemaking?

In contemplating a future without Arafat, it is valuable to note the words of Dennis Ross, a figure at the heart of US peacemaking efforts for more than a decade. In his hefty account of these times, *The Missing Peace*, Ross rightly excoriated Arafat for his inability to risk the transition from revolutionary to statesman. But he also offered telling commentary on the underlying mentality of the conflict. Ross observed the reluctance of each side to acknowledge the legitimacy of the other's grievances and needs, the unwillingness to confront comfortable myths, to acknowledge mistakes, or to change behaviour. The Israelis, Ross wrote, 'acted as if all decisions should be informed by their needs, not by possible Palestinian needs or reactions'. On the other side, he said, the transformation that would make it possible 'to acknowledge that Israel has needs' had not taken place.

Arafat certainly helped to foster this mentality. But his disappearance from the scene will not miraculously erase it. On hearing of Arafat's death, Tommy Lapid, then Israel's Minister for Justice, proclaimed a new era of sunshine in the Middle East. More sober and realistic commentators recognised that the not-entirely dear departed had left a long shadow. Yossi Alpher, former director of the Jaffee Center for Strategic Studies in Tel Aviv, contemplated 'a worst-case scenario' in which parts of Palestine would 'resemble Somalia, with Hamas ruling most of Gaza, Fatah dissidents controlling the northern West Bank, and the mainstream PLO in Ramallah'. Barry Rubin, Israeli academic and trenchant Arafat critic, warned that, despite the claim 'that a moderate trend offers opportunity for advancing peace', the reality on the Palestinian side was one of minimal civil order, division, and possible Hamas veto power. The main question was not who but what would replace Arafat. 'The paradox here,' Rubin wrote,

> is that while Arafat ... refused to make peace, the vacuum left by his passing may not make that task any easier ... With no-one clearly in charge — and rivals trying to outbid each other by proving their legitimacy through militancy ... there will be no one whose authority or action is going to convince Israelis to make concessions or take risks.

The building — or stumbling — blocks of any future Israeli-Palestinian settlement did not change on 11 November 2004. Mkhaimar Abusada, professor of political science at Gaza's Al-Azhar University, commented that

Arafat set forth a blueprint including an independent state in the West Bank and Gaza, with East Jerusalem as its capital, and a fair and just solution to the refugee problem. Changing leaders will in no way alter these conditions for making peace.

Writing for the Yale Center for the Study of Globalization, Rami Khouri, executive editor of Lebanon's *Daily Star* newspaper, suggested that it was

naïve to assume that a post-Arafat leadership would give in meekly to most American and Israeli demands. The personalities will change in Palestine, and tactical approaches to peace-making will become more flexible, but substantive policies of the Palestinians will not differ.

In Arafat's last years, Israel cited his obduracy and untrustworthiness as the principal impediment to peace. The claimed lack of a Palestinian 'peace partner' provided Sharon with the freedom to pursue unilateral 'disengagement': the planned withdrawal of Israeli settlers from Gaza and the token settler relocation in the West Bank. Without a Palestinian 'peace partner', Sharon did largely as he wished, his main impediment being the fractious nature of Israeli domestic politics.

The potential for future Israeli excuses for action or inaction seem limitless: a weak and uncertain Palestinian leadership; failure of the Palestinians to democratise or, conversely, an excessive democratisation which strengthens the role of Islamists; continuing, if diminished, Palestinian violence; or

Palestinian intransigence over the principle of a fully fledged right of return for Palestinian refugees. And for Palestinians, will Israel's continuing occupation and settlement activity provide an easy rationale for killing rather than talking, strengthened by Palestinian indignation — real or feigned — over Israeli retaliation for Palestinian terrorist attacks?

On what basis could the parties restart negotiations? One option would be the American-devised proposals of late 2000: Palestinian control of Palestinian neighbourhoods in East Jerusalem; all of Gaza; around 95 per cent of the West Bank (with some territorial compensation for West Bank land remaining under Israeli control); and a compromise solution over Palestinian refugees. Arafat was unable to say yes to this package, partly because of a failure of imagination and nerve, partly because the negotiation process itself was seriously flawed. Would a post-Arafat leadership agree to anything less? And would Israelis now contemplate anything remotely approaching this?

Will Palestinians feel any less the victims because of Arafat's disappearance? Will Israelis feel any more confident about the Palestinian leadership's commitment to fight extremism and its capacity to do so? Will there be any greater trust in the other's word and capacity to deliver? If the Israelis do not trust the Palestinians, they will be loath to make the 'concessions' of giving up occupied territory or curbing settlement growth. If the Palestinians do not trust the Israelis, they will be loath to mothball the use or the threat of violence.

And if the parties do not trust each other it cannot be

imposed, whether by the US, the UN, or anyone. Dennis Ross has written that, during the ultimately futile negotiations in 2000, 'I wanted to address what each side needed, not what it wanted and not what they felt they were entitled to.' He does not explain how he came to determine each side's precise 'needs'. It seems a remarkable proposition that any outsider, even the US, could do so. And for the US there is another, larger, issue. Can it rid itself of the image that it is there primarily to protect Israeli interests: that it can move, as Rami Khouri has put it, to work 'vigorously for a fair, negotiated Arab-Israeli peace ... that responds equally to Israeli, Palestinian, and other Arab rights', reducing terror though political and economic means 'rather than primarily through military policies designed largely by pro-Israeli ideologues in Washington'?

Israelis and Palestinians and those who support them — whether blindly or impartially — know what is required in the post-Arafat world. Both sides seek secure, viable statehood. But it is one thing to know; an entirely different thing to do. Israelis and Palestinians struggle to bring themselves to accept, openly and unequivocally, the legitimacy of the other's minimal requirements. They struggle to renounce their competing dreams — either a land freed of Jews or freed of Palestinians. They play games with each other and indeed with us all. They accept the principle of peacemaking but not the compromises, physical and mental, needed to achieve this, always conveniently blaming the other. Their conflict and the struggle to divide the tiny land they both call home will go on. And it will go on making our world a nasty and dangerous place.

Notes

Introduction: One hundred years of living painfully

1   Except where otherwise indicated, the term 'Israeli' refers to the
    80 per cent of Israelis who are Jews.

Chapter One: Herzl's 'new' Jew versus the 'semi-savage' native

1   As were others. In his 2004 book on Stalin, Donald Rayfield notes
    that, for a time, the Crimea was a possibility: 'In the 1920s and
    1930s some $30 million had been contributed by Americans to
    aid Jewish settlers in the north Crimean steppes. Molotov was
    dubious: he thought Jews an urban people who "couldn't be put
    on a tractor". '

Chapter Two: Zionism triumphant

1   The 'revisionist' or 'new' historians have challenged key founding
    myths of Israel. They argue that force was used deliberately to
    drive Palestinians away and that the military odds were not
    stacked against the new state.
2   Ironically, a few Zionist hardliners also contemplated seeking
    Nazi assistance against the British.

Chapter Three: This land is my land; your land is my land

1   'The Bloc of the Faithful.'
2   The Israeli Government does not publish its spending on the set-
    tlements. This figure comes from an investigation by the highly
    respected *Ha'aretz* newspaper.
3   In *Beyond Peace: the Search for Security in the Middle East*, Robert
    Bowker noted one study which suggested that Israeli settlers in

the West Bank used at least three times as much water per capita as the Palestinians.

Chapter Four: Blood ... talk ... blood

1 The reverse of the Arabic acronym for the 'Movement for the Liberation of Palestine'.

2 Fill half a bottle with tar, lime or turpentine oil. To the tar add a quantity of benzine, about a quarter of the bottle's capacity. Now add an additional quantity of oil to the mixture, equal to half the quantity of benzine. Take a caulker and place it around several matches, side by side, turning the heads of the matches up, outside the bottle. Seal the bottle properly. To operate it, light one of the matches and throw the bottle at the target.

3 Hamas is an acronym from the Arabic for the 'Islamic Resistance Movement'.

4 Not quite; he had to leave his gun outside and sported an empty holster.

5 The Human Rights Watch report, *Erased in a Moment*, offered the following conclusion:

> High-ranking PA officials, including President Arafat, failed in their duty to administer justice and enforce the rule of law ... Through their repeated failure to arrest or prosecute individuals alleged to have planned or carried out suicide attacks against civilians, they contributed to a climate of impunity — and failed to prevent the bloody consequences. Their payments to, and recruitment of, individuals responsible for attacks against civilians likewise demonstrate, at least, a serious failure to meet their political responsibilities as the governing authorities ... However, there is no publicly available evidence that Arafat or other senior PA officials ordered, planned, or carried out such attacks.

Chapter Five: Whither the Zionist enterprise?

1 During his time as chief of staff of Israel's northern sector,

Sharon once asked his staff to gather data on the number of vehicles required to transport the entire Arab population of the region to neighbouring Arab countries in the event of war with Syria.

2   Elsewhere, Christison has argued that the notion of the superiority of Jewish history and destiny over its Palestinian counterpart has governed popular thinking, media commentary, and policy making in the US. 'We understand Israeli fears; we feel Israeli fears. But we generally don't feel, or even care about, Palestinian fears. We have no conception of what it means for a Palestinian to have his land confiscated, his olive grove bulldozed, his underground water sucked up, so that Israel can build a settlement for Jews only or a security road on which only Israelis are allowed to drive.'

Chapter Six: Palestinian fantasies

1   Not *the* territories, which provided plenty of room for argument about what the resolutions actually intended.

2   Not quite: Menachem Begin's Etzel movement, for example, had blown up the British Embassy in Rome, and Britain's Lord Moyne was shot in Cairo by two members of Lehi.

3   *Palestinian Refugees and the Politics of Peacemaking.*

Selected reading

Geoffrey Aronson, *Israel, Palestinians and the Intifada: Creating Facts on the West Bank*, Kegan Paul International, 1990.

Robert Bowker, *Beyond Peace: the Search for Security in the Middle East*, Lynne Rienne Publishers, 1996.

Roane Carey/Jonathan Shainin (editors), *The Other Israel — Voices of Refusal and Dissent*, The New Press, 2002.

Yaron Ezrahi, *Rubber Bullets — Power and Conscience in Modern Israel*, Farrar, Straus and Giroux, 1997.

Shlomo Gazit, *Trapped Fools: Thirty Years of Israeli Policy in the Territories*, Portland/Frank Cass, 2003.

Theodor Herzl, *The Jewish State*, translated by Sylie D'Avigdor, Zionist Organisation, 1934.

Theodor Herzl, *Zionist Writings: Essays and Addresses,* volumes one and two, translated by Harry Zohn, Herzl Press, 1973, 1975.

David Horovitz, *Still Life With Bombers: Israel in the Age of Terrorism*, Knopf, 2004.

Efraim Karsh, *Arafat's War — The Man and His Battle for Israeli Conquest*, Grove Press, 2003.

Efraim Karsh, *Fabricating Israeli History — The 'New Historians'*, Frank Cass, 2000.

Richard Ben Kramer, *How Israel Lost – The Four Questions*, Simon and Schuster, 2004.

Nur Masalha, *Land Without a People: Israel, Transfer and the Palestinians 1949–96*, Faber, 1997.

Benny Morris, *The Birth of the Palestinian Refugee Problem Revisited*, Cambridge University Press, 2004.

Benny Morris, *Righteous Victims – A History of the Zionist-Arab Conflict, 1881–1999*, Alfred Knopf, 1999.

Barry Rubin/Judith Colp Rubin, *Yasir Arafat: a Political Biography*, OUP, 2003.

Danny Rubinstein, *The People of Nowhere – The Palestinian Vision of Home*, Times Books, 1991.

Tom Segev, *One Palestine Complete — Jews and Arabs Under the British Mandate*, Metropolitan Books, 2000.

Avi Shlaim, *The Iron Wall: Israel and the Arab World*, Norton, 2000.

Leonard Weinberg & Ami Pedahzur (editors), *Religious Fundamentalism and Political Extremism*, Frank Cass, 2004.

Andrew Wheatley, *The Controversy of Zion*, Addison Wesley, 1996.

The Corporation
The Pathological Pursuit of Profit and Power

Joel Bakan
£6.99, 1-84529-174-3

Required by law to maximize returns to share-
holders, the publicly traded corporation enjoys
an inhuman clarity of purpose. As Bakan argues
in what is both a diagnosis and a course of
treatment, it is time to see corporations for
what they are, and to take steps to defend ourselves against them.

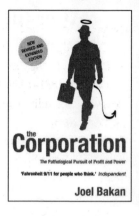

Praise for *The Corporation*

'The opposite of a blunderbuss-wielding Michael Moore, Bakan is a
Canadian law professor whose brief is as well-ordered, concise and sober
as the accusation is grave: behind its benevolent face, the most important
institution of modern capitalism is a Frankenstein's monster that has
broken its chains and is now consuming the society that created it.'
Simon Caulkin, *Observer*

'No matter how cuddly and cute big business pretends to be, in the end it
loves money much more than it loves you. Wake up and smell *The
Corporation.*'
Stephen Applebaum, *Sunday Herald*

'Unlike much of the soggy thinking peddled by too many anti-globalisers,
The Corporation is a surprisingly rational and coherent attack on
capitalism's most important institution.'
The Economist

'This fine book was virtually begging to be written. With lucidity and
verve, expert knowledge and incisive analysis, Bakan unveils the history
and character of a devilish instrument that has been created and is
nurtured by modern states.'
Noam Chomsky

'*Fahrenheit 9/11* for people who think.'
Johann Hari, *Independent*

After the Empire

The Breakdown of the American Order

Emmanuel Todd

£8.99, 1-84529-058-5

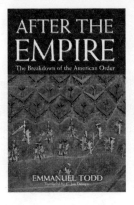

In 1975, Emmanuel Todd predicted the decline and fall of the Soviet Union, drawing on research from cultural anthropology and demography as well as from economics. At the time his findings challenged a conventional wisdom that saw in the Communist world a dynamic and growing challenge to the West. Generations of Kremlinologists may not have known much but they knew that Todd was wrong – until 1989, that is, when conventional wisdom retired hurt.

Now Todd returns to the debate on the future of international power relations with another startling prediction. Far from being at the apogee of its power, the United States of America is now locked in the messy and disruptive logic of decline. Although the world has long relied on America as a source of stability, it is now desperately important for us to find a way to contain the shock waves from America's impending collapse as the sole superpower.

This is not a book from an anti-American, and you will not find a smooth recitation of the standard arguments of Left or Right. It is that unfashionable thing, a determined and unembarrassed attempt to tell the truth.

Praise for *After the Empire*

'A brave and challenging book with a great deal of truth in it.'

Clare Short, *New Statesman*

'A refreshing piece of dissent.'   *Sunday Times*

'A powerful antidote to hysterical exaggeration of American power and potential by American triumphalists and anti-American polemicists alike'

Michael Lind, author of *Made in Texas:
George W. Bush and the Takeover of American Politics*